BIGGLES LE

*The sky around Biggles became an
inferno of darting flames and hurtling
metal. Suddenly, the shadow that was
the earth swept up to meet him. He
lifted his knees to his chin, covered his
face with his arms, and waited for the
end . . .*

Plunged into the horrors of war at just
seventeen, Biggles has to learn quickly if
he is to stay alive in the Royal Flying
Corps. And with dangerous missions
over enemy lines against formidable
opposition, wartime flying is hardly the
thrilling game which the young Biggles
had expected . . .

The very first Biggles adventure

Copyright © the estate of the late
W. E. Johns

First published in the U.K. in
1935 by Boy's Friend Library

Knight Books edition 1986
Third impression 1988

British Library C.I.P.

Johns, W. E. (William Earl)
  Biggles learns to fly
  I. Title
  823'.912[J]   PZ7

  ISBN 0-340-38842-0

Printed and bound in Great
Britain for Hodder and Stoughton
Paperbacks, a division of Hodder
and Stoughton Ltd., Mill Road,
Dunton Green, Sevenoaks, Kent
TN13 2YA. (Editorial Office: 47
Bedford Square, London WC1B
3DP) by Richard Clay Ltd.,
Bungay, Suffolk

Biggles Learns to Fly

Captain W. E. Johns

KNIGHT BOOKS
Hodder and Stoughton

BIGGLES FROM THE START

THE printing of this book is the answer to those who have asked when and where Biggles learned to fly. It was written many years ago, while the events were fresh in the author's mind, long before there was any talk of Hitler and a second World War. The sons of some of the boys who read it then now fly jets. Time marches on—and in aviation it has marched very fast indeed. But this was the beginning, and the beginning of Biggles.

To readers of the modern Biggles books these early adventures may seem strange, both in the terms used and in the style of conversation. But Biggles was very young then. So was the Air Service. In fact, there was no air service. Fighting 'planes were flown by officers seconded from the Army (the R.F.C.) and the Navy (Royal Naval Air Service).

When Biggles (and the author) learned to fly, aeroplanes and equipment, by modern standards, were primitive. Combat tactics, as they are understood to-day, were unknown. Every pilot had his own method and, if he lived long enough, picked up a few tricks from the old hands. Once in the air he could more or less do as he pleased, for he was out of touch with the ground except by simple visual signals.

Communication between aircraft, or between pilot and gunner, was also by hand signals. Crossed fingers meant an enemy aircraft. First finger and thumb in the form of a circle meant British aircraft. Thumbs up meant all was well. Thumbs down—well, not so good. One also signalled the approach of enemy aircraft by rocking one's wings.

As the reader may guess, the writer's own experiences were much the same as those described herein. A few flights, and off you went solo. A few hours solo, and off you went to war, to take your luck. Casualties, of course, were grim; but all the same, happy-go-lucky were those days that have now become history. The mystery is that anyone survived, for apart from the risks of battle, structural failure was common, and there were no parachutes. On the other hand, the machines being slow, and made of wood, wire and fabric, one had a better chance in a crash than in the modern high-performance fighter.

Here are some explanatory notes:

SOPWITH PUP   Scout type biplane with a rotary engine. The last word in 1916.

SOPWITH CAMEL	A more powerful development of the Pup, but tricky to fly.
BRISTOL FIGHTER	A very efficient two-seater all-purpose machine that remained standard equipment in the R.A.F. for many years.
F.E.2B	A two-seater 'pusher' type used extensively in the 1914-18 war. The pilot sat in front of the engine with the gunner in front of him. With a more powerful engine it became the F.E.2D.
L.V.G.	A German two-seater, the product of Luft Verkehrs Gesellschaft.
ALBATROS	An efficient German fighter. (English, Albatross.)
TRIPLANE	The Fokker Triplane was used by many of the leading German aces. Often referred to as a Tripe, or Tripehound.
JAGDSTAFFEL	German fighter unit. Literally, a hunting squadron.
ARCHIE	Anti-aircraft fire. In the last war it was 'flak'.
POUR THE SAUCE	French slang for 'open the throttle'.
A SITTER	A machine flying directly away—an easy mark.
FLAMING ONIONS	A type of German anti-aircraft shell thus nicknamed by British pilots.
BLAZE	The strip of burnt grass in front of the muzzle of a heavy gun.
B.I.s	Baby Incendiary bombs. They were thrown out of the cockpit by hand—a dangerous game.
JAMPOT	Slang for an engine cylinder.
COLD MEAT	An easy victim.

The word 'Hun', as used in this book, was the common generic term for anything belonging to the enemy. It was used in a familiar sense, rather than derogatory. Witness the fact that in the R.F.C. a hun was also a pupil at a flying training school.

W.E.J.

First Time Up!

ONE FINE LATE September morning in the war-stricken year of 1916, a young officer, in the distinctive uniform of the Royal Flying Corps, appeared in the doorway of one of the long, low, narrow wooden huts which, mushroom-like, had sprung up all over England during the previous eighteen months. He paused for a moment to regard a great open expanse that stretched away as far as he could see before him in the thin autumn mist that made everything outside a radius of a few hundred yards seem shadowy and vague.

There was little about him to distinguish him from thousands of others in whose ears the call to arms had not sounded in vain, and who were doing precisely the same thing in various parts of the country. His uniform was still free from the marks of war that would eventually stain it. His Sam Browne belt still squeaked slightly when he moved, like a pair of new boots.

There was nothing remarkable, or even martial, about his physique; on the contrary, he was slim, rather below average height, and delicate-looking. A wisp of fair hair protruded from one side of his rakishly tilted R.F.C. cap; his eyes, now sparkling with pleasurable anticipation, were what is usually called hazel. His features were finely cut, but the squareness of his chin and the firm line of his mouth revealed a certain doggedness, a tenacity of purpose, that denied any suggestion of weakness. Only his hands were small and white, and might have been those of a girl.

His youthfulness was apparent. He might have reached the eighteen years shown on his papers, but his birth certificate, had he produced it at the recruiting office, would have

7

revealed that he would not attain that age for another eleven months. Like many others who had left school to plunge straight into the war, he had conveniently 'lost' his birth certificate when applying for enlistment, nearly three months previously.

A heavy, hair-lined leather coat, which looked large enough for a man twice his size, hung stiffly over his arm. In his right hand he held a flying-helmet, also of leather but lined with fur, a pair of huge gauntlets, with coarse, yellowish hair on the backs, and a pair of goggles.

He started as the silence was shattered by a reverberating roar which rose to a mighty crescendo and then died away to a low splutter. The sound, which he knew was the roar of an aero-engine, although he had never been so close to one before, came from a row of giant structures that loomed dimly through the now-dispersing mist, along one side of the bleak expanse upon which he gazed with eager anticipation. There was little enough to see, yet he had visualized that flat area of sandy soil, set with short, coarse grass, a thousand times during the past two months while he had been at the 'ground' school. It was an aerodrome, or, to be more precise, the aerodrome of No. 17 Flying Training School, which was situated near the village of Settling, in Norfolk. The great, darkly looming buildings were the hangars that housed the extraordinary collection of hastily built aeroplanes which at this period of the first Great War were used to teach pupils the art of flying.

A faint smell was borne to his nostrils, a curious aroma that brought a slight flush to his cheeks. It was one common to all aerodromes, a mingling of petrol, oil, dope, and burnt gases, and which, once experienced, was never forgotten.

Figures, all carrying flying-kit, began to emerge from other huts and hurry towards the hangars, where strange-looking vehicles were now being wheeled out on to a strip of concrete that shone whitely along the front of the hangars for their entire length. After a last appraising glance around, the new officer set off at a brisk pace in their direction.

A chilly breeze had sprung up; it swept aside the curtain

of mist and exposed the white orb of the sun, low in the sky, for it was still very early. Yet it was daylight, and no daylight was wasted at flying schools during the Great War.

He reached the nearest hangar, and then stopped, eyes devouring an extraordinary structure of wood, wire, and canvas that stood in his path. A propeller, set behind two exposed seats, revolved slowly. Beside it stood a tall, thin man in flying-kit; his leather flying-coat, which was filthy beyond description with oil stains, flapped open, exposing an equally dirty tunic, on the breast of which a device in the form of a small pair of wings could just be seen. Under them was a tiny strip of the violet-and-white ribbon of the Military Cross.

To a fully fledged pilot the figure would have been commonplace enough, but the young newcomer regarded him with an awe that amounted almost to worship. He knew that the tall, thin man could fly; not only could he fly, but he had fought other aeroplanes in the sky, as the decoration on his breast proved. At that moment, however, he seemed merely bored, for he yawned mightily as he stared at the aeroplane with no sign of interest. Then, turning suddenly, he saw the newcomer watching him.

'You one of the fellows on the new course?' he asked shortly.

'Er—er—yes, sir,' was the startled reply.

'Ever been in the air?'

'No, sir.'

'What's your name?'

'Bigglesworth, sir. I'm afraid it's a bit of a mouthful, but that isn't my fault. Most people call me Biggles for short.'

A slow smile spread over the face of the instructor.

'Sensible idea,' he said. 'All right, Biggles, get in.'

Biggles started violently. He knew that he had come to the aerodrome to learn to fly, but at the back of his mind he had an idea that there would be some sort of ceremony about it, some preliminary overtures that would slowly lead up to a grand finale in which he would take his place in an aeroplane before the eyes of admiring mechanics. And now the instructor had just said 'Get in!' as if the aeroplane were a common motor-car. Mechanics were there, it is true, but they were getting on with their work, taking not the slightest notice of the thrilling exploit about to be enacted. Only one, a corporal, was standing near the nose of the machine looking round the sky with a half-vacant expression on his face.

In something like a daze, Biggles donned his flying-kit. It was the first time he had worn it, and he felt that the weight of it would bear him to the ground. Stiffly he approached the machine.

'Look out!'

He sprang back as the shrill warning came faintly to his ears through the thick helmet. The instructor was glaring at him, his face convulsed with rage.

'What are you trying to do?' he roared. 'Break my propeller with your head? Come round to the front!'

'Sorry, sir,' gasped Biggles, and hurried as fast as his heavy kit would permit to the front of the machine. He raised his foot and clutched at a wire to help him up.

'Not there, you fool! Take your foot off that wing before you burst the fabric!' shouted the instructor from his seat.

Biggles backed away hastily—too hastily; his foot caught in one of the many wires that ran in all directions. He clutched wildly at the leading edge of the lower 'plane to save himself, but in vain, and the next instant he had measured his length on the ground.

The instructor looked down at him with such withering contempt that Biggles nearly burst into tears. The corporal came to his assistance. 'Put your left foot in that hole—now the other one in there—now swing yourself up. That's right!'

To Biggles the cockpit seemed hopelessly inadequate, but he squeezed himself into it somehow and settled down with a sigh of relief. Something struck him smartly on the back of the head, and he jumped violently.

'Strap in,' said a hard voice, 'and keep your hands and feet off the controls. If you start any nonsense I'll lam you over the back of the skull with this!'

With some difficulty Biggles screwed his head round to see what 'this' was. A large iron wrench was thrust under his nose; at the same moment the machine began to move forward, slowly at first, but with ever-increasing speed.

Something like panic seized him, and he struggled wildly to buckle up the cumbrous leather belt that he could see on either side of him. It took him a minute to realize that he was sitting on it. 'If he loops the loop or something I'm sunk!' he muttered bitterly, as he fought to pull it from under him. The machine seemed to lurch suddenly, and he grabbed both sides of the cockpit, looking down as he did so. The hangars were just disappearing below.

The next few minutes, which seemed an hour, were a nightmare. The machine rose and fell in a series of sickening movements; every now and then one of the wings would tip up at an alarming angle. He was capable of one thought only: 'I shall never fly this thing as long as I live—never. I must have been crazy to think I could.'

Woods, fields, and houses passed below in bewildering succession, each looking like its fellow. Had the pilot told him they were over any county in the United Kingdom, he would have believed him.

'We must have gone fifty miles away from the aerodrome,' he thought presently; but the nose of the machine tilted down, and he saw the hangars leaping up towards him. For a moment he really did not believe they were the hangars; he thought it was a trick of the imagination. But there was a sudden grinding of wheels, and before he really grasped what was happening, the machine had run to a standstill in exactly the same spot from which it had taken off. He surveyed the apparent miracle with wonderment, making no effort to move.

'Well, how did you like it?' said a voice in his ear.

Biggles clambered awkwardly from his seat and turned to the speaker. The instructor was actually smiling.

'Grand!' he cried enthusiastically. 'Top hole.'

'Didn't feel sick?'

'Not a bit.'

'It's a wonder. It's bumpy enough to make anyone sick; we shall have to pack up flying if it doesn't get better. Let's go and mark your time up on the board. Enter up your log-book "First flight. Air experience five minutes." '

'Five minutes!' cried Biggles incredulously. 'Were we only up five minutes? I thought we were at least half an hour.'

The instructor had stopped before a notice-board headed ' "A" Flight,' below which was a list of names.

'What did you say your name was?' he asked, a frown lining his forehead.

'Bigglesworth, sir.'

'What flight are you in?'

'Flight? I don't know, sir.'

'You don't know?' snarled the instructor. 'Then what the dickens do you mean by wasting my time? What were you loafing about here for? These are "A" Flight sheds.'

Biggles stepped back quickly in his nervousness; his heel struck a chock, and he grabbed wildly at a passing officer to save himself from falling.

'Hi! Not so much of the clutching hand!' growled a voice. 'This is a flying ground, not a wrestling school.'

'Sorry!' cried Biggles, aghast, detaching himself.

'Your name isn't Bigglesworth, by any chance, is it?' went on the officer, a short, thick-set man with a frightful scar on his face that reached from the corner of one eye to his chin.

'Why, yes, sir,' replied Biggles hesitatingly.

'Then what are you doing down here? You're in my flight, and you've kept the class waiting.'

'I've been flying, sir,' protested Biggles.

'You've been what?'

'He's right!' grumbled the first instructor. 'He was down here, so I naturally thought he was one of my fellows. I wish you'd look after your own pupils!'

Biggles waited for no more, but hurried along the tarmac to where a little group of officers—all pupils, judging by their spotless uniforms—stood at the door of a hangar.

'Where have you been?' cried one. 'Nerky's been blinding you to all eternity!'

'Nerky?'

'Captain Nerkinson. We call him Nerky because he's as nerky as they make 'em! He's crashed about ten times, so you can't blame him. Look out, here he comes!'

12

'Well, don't let us waste any more time,' began the instructor. 'Gather round this machine while I tell you something about it.'

The pupils formed a respectful semi-circle round the machine he had indicated.

'This aeroplane,' he began, 'is called a Maurice Farman Shorthorn, chiefly because it hasn't any horns, short or otherwise. Some people call it a Rumpity. Others call it a bird-cage, because of the number of wires it has got. The easiest way to find out if all the wires are in their places is to put a canary between the wings; if the bird gets out, you know there is a wire missing somewhere.

'Always remember that if this machine gets into a spin, it never gets out of it; and if it gets into a dive, the wings are apt to come off. Presently I shall take you up in it, one at a time; if anybody doesn't like it, he has only to say so, and he can transfer to the infantry.'

His voice trailed away to a whisper as a faint whistling sound reached their ears. All eyes were staring upwards at a machine that was coming in to land. It was a Rumpity, and it seemed to be descending in short jerks, as if coming down an invisible staircase; the pilot could be seen sitting bolt upright in his seat.

A deep groan burst from the instructor's lips, as if he had been suddenly smitten with a violent pain.

'That's Rafferty, I'll bet my hide!' he muttered. 'I thought I'd cured him of that habit. Watch him, everybody, and you'll see the answer to the question why instructors go mad!'

Everybody on the tarmac was watching the machine, Biggles with a curious mixture of fear and fascination. A motor-truck, with a dozen mechanics carrying Pyrene fire-extinguishers hanging on to it, was already moving out on to the aerodrome in anticipation of the crash.

The pilot of the descending machine continued to swoop downwards in a series of short jerks. At the last moment he seemed to realize his danger, and must have pulled the joy-stick back into his stomach, for the machine reared up like a startled horse and then slid back, tail first, to the ground. There was a terrific crash of breaking woodwork and tearing fabric, and the machine collapsed in a cloud of flying splinters. The pilot shot out of his seat as if propelled by an invisible spring, and rolled over and over along the the ground like a shot rabbit. Then, to the utter astonishment of everybody, he rose to his feet and rubbed the back of his head ruefully. A shout of laughter rose into the air from the spectators.

Captain Nerkinson nodded soberly.

'You have just seen a beautiful picture,' he said, 'of how not to land an aeroplane!'

Landed—but Lost

A WEEK LATER, a Rumpity landed on the aerodrome, and
Captain Nerkinson swung himself to the ground. Biggles,
in the front cockpit, was about to follow, but the instructor
stopped him.

'You're absolutely O.K.,' he said, 'except that you are
inclined to come in a bit too fast. Don't forget that. Off
you go!'

'Off I what?' cried Biggles, refusing to believe his ears.

'You heard me. You're as right as rain—but don't be
more than ten minutes.'

'I won't—by James I won't, you can bet your life on
that!' declared Biggles emphatically. He took a last linger-
ing survey of the aerodrome, as when a swimmer who has
climbed up to the high diving-board for the first time looks
down. Then, suddenly making up his mind, he thrust the
throttle open with a despairing jerk and grabbed at the
weird, spectacle-like arrangement that served as a joy-
stick in the Rumpity.

The machine leapt forward and careered wildly in a
wide circle towards the distant hedge. For a moment, as
the machine started to swing, Biggles thought he was going to turn a complete circle and charge the hangars; but
he kept his head, and straightened it.

The tail lifted, and he eased the joy-stick back gently.
To his surprise the machine lifted as lightly as a feather,
but the needle on the air-speed indicator ran back alarm-
ingly. He shoved the joy-stick forward again with a frantic
movement as he realized with a heart-palpitating shock that
he had nearly stalled through climbing too quickly. Settling

15

his nose on the horizon and holding the machine on an even keel, he soon began to gather confidence.

A nasty 'bump' over the edge of a wood brought his heart into his mouth, and he muttered 'Whoa, there!' as if he was talking to a horse. The sound of his own voice increased his confidence, so from time to time he encouraged himself with such comments as 'Steady, there! Whoa, my beauty!' and 'Easy does it!'

Presently it struck him that it was time he started turning to complete a circuit that would bring him back to the aerodrome. He snatched a swift glance over his left shoulder, but he could not see the hangars. He turned a little farther and looked again. The aerodrome was nowhere in sight. It had disappeared as completely as if the earth had opened and swallowed it up. Perspiration broke out on his brow as he quickened his turn and examined every point of the compass in quick succession; but there was no aerodrome.

It took him another few seconds to realize that this miracle had actually taken place.

'No matter,' he muttered. 'I've only got to go back the way I came and I can't miss it.' In five minutes he was looking down on country that he knew he had never seen before.

His heart fluttered, and his lips turned dry as the full shock of the fact that he was completely lost struck him. Another 'plane appeared in his range of vision, seeming to drift sideways like a great grasshopper in that curious manner other machines have in the air, and he followed it eagerly. It might not be going to his aerodrome, but that did not matter; any aerodrome would suit him equally well. His toe slipped off the rudder-bar, and he looked down to adjust it.

When he looked up again his machine was in an almost vertical bank; he levelled out from a sickening side-slip, with beads of moisture forming inside his goggles. He pushed them up with a nervous jerk, and looked around for the other machine. It had gone. North, south, east and west he strained his eyes, but in vain. His heart sank, but he spotted a railway line and headed towards it.

16

'It must be the line that goes to Settling,' he thought, and he started to follow it eagerly. He was quite right—it was; but unfortunately he was going in the wrong direction.

After what seemed an eternity of time, a curious phenomenon appeared ahead. It seemed as if the land stopped short, ending abruptly in space, so to speak. He pondered it for a moment, and had just arrived at the conclusion that it was a belt of fog, when something else caught his eye, and he stared at it wonderingly. The shape seemed familiar, but for a moment or two he could not make out what it was. It looked like a ship, but how could a ship float in fog? Other smaller ones came into view, and at last the truth dawned on him. He was looking at the sea. It seemed impossible. As near as he could judge by visualizing the map, the coast was at least forty miles from Settling.

'This is frightful!' he groaned, and turned away from the forbidding spectacle. A blast of air smote him on the cheek, and objects on the ground suddenly grew larger. He clenched his teeth, knowing that he had side-slipped badly on the turn. He snatched a quick glance at the altimeter, and noted that it indicated four hundred feet, whereas a moment before the needle had pointed to the twelve hundred mark.

'Good heavens, this won't do!' he told himself angrily. 'What was it Nerky had said? "Never lose your head!" That was it.' He pulled himself together with an effort and looked at his watch. He had been in the air an hour and a half, and Nerky had told him not to be more than ten minutes.

He wondered how much longer his petrol would last, realizing with fresh dismay that he did not know how much petrol had been in the tanks when he started. The light was already failing; presently it would be dark, and what hope would he have then of finding his way? He remembered that he had a map in his pocket, but what use was that if he did not know where he was? He could only find that out by landing and asking somebody.

'It's the only way!' he told himself despairingly. 'I might

go on drifting round in circles for the rest of my life without finding the aerodrome.'

He began to watch the ground for a suitable field on which to land.

He flew for some time before he found one. It was an enormous field, beautifully green, and he headed the machine towards it. At the last moment it struck him that there was something queer about the grass, and he pulled up again with a jerk, realizing that he had nearly landed on a field of turnips. .

Another quarter of an hour passed, and another large field presented itself; it looked like stubble, which could do the machine no harm; but he approached it warily. Only when he was quite sure that it was stubble did he pull the throttle back. The sudden silence as the engine died away almost frightened him, and he watched the ground, now seeming to come towards him, longingly.

In the next few seconds of agonizing suspense he hardly knew what he did, and it was with unspeakable relief and surprise that he heard his wheels trundling over solid earth. The machine stopped, and he surveyed the countryside, scarcely able to believe that he was actually on the ground.

'I've landed!' he told himself joyfully. 'Landed without breaking anything! How did I do it? Good old aeroplane!' he went on, patting the wooden side of the cockpit. 'You must have done it yourself—I didn't. But the thing is, where are we?'

He stood up in the cockpit and looked around. Not a soul was in sight, nor was there any sign of human habitation.

'I would choose the only place in England where there aren't any roads, houses or people!' he thought bitterly. 'If I've got to walk to the horizon looking for somebody, it will be pitch dark before I get back. Then I should probably lose myself as well as the aeroplane!' he concluded miserably.

He sprang up as the sound of an aero engine reached his ears. It was a Rumpity, and, what was more, it was coming towards him. It almost looked as if the pilot intended landing in the same field.

18

'Cheers!' muttered Biggles. 'Now I shall soon know where I am!'

He was quite right; he was soon to know.

The Rumpity landed. The pilot jumped to the ground and strode towards him; there seemed to be something curiously familar about his gait.

'Can it be?' thought Biggles. 'Great jumping fish, it is. Well, I'm dashed!'

Captain Nerkinson, his brows black as a thunder-cloud, was coming toward him. 'What game d'you think you're playing?' he snarled.

'Game?' echoed Biggles, in amazement. 'Playing?'

'Yes, game! Who told you you could land outside the aerodrome?'

'I told myself,' replied Biggles truthfully. 'I wanted to find out where I was. I lost myself, and I knew I had got so far away from the aerodrome that I——'

'Lost! What are you talking about? You've crossed the aerodrome three times during the last hour. I saw you!'

'I crossed the aerodrome?'

'You've just flown straight over it! That's why I chased you.'

'Flown over it!' Biggles shut his eyes, and shook his head, shuddering. 'Then it can only be a few miles away,' he exclaimed.

'A few miles! It's only a few yards, you young fool— just the other side of the hedge!'

Biggles sank down weakly in his seat.

'All right, let's get back,' went on the instructor. 'Follow close behind, and don't take your eyes off me.'

He hurried back to his machine and took off. Biggles followed. The leading machine merely hopped over the hedge and then began to glide down again at once, and Biggles could hardly believe his eyes when the aerodrome loomed up; it did not seem possible that he could have missed seeing those enormous sheds.

He started to glide down in Captain Nerkinson's wake.

He seemed to be travelling much faster than the leading machine, for his nose was soon nearly touching its tail. He saw the instructor lean out of his seat and look back at him, white-faced. He seemed to be yelling something.

'He thinks I'm going to ram him,' thought Biggles. 'And so I shall if he doesn't get out of my way; he ought to know jolly well that I can't stop.'

The instructor landed, but he did not stop; instead, he raced madly across the ground towards the far side of the aerodrome, Biggles following close behind.

'I'm not losing you,' he declared grimly.

Captain Nerkinson swung round in a wide circle towards the sheds, and then, leaping out of the machine almost before it had stopped, sprinted for safety.

Biggles missed the other machine by inches; indeed, he would probably have crashed into it but for half a dozen mechanics, who, seeing the danger, dashed out and grabbed his wings.

'Are you trying to kill me?' Captain Nerkinson asked him, with deadly calm. He was breathing heavily.

'You said I wasn't to lose you.'

'I know I did, but I didn't ask you to ram me, you lunatic!'

The instructor recovered himself, and pointed to the hangar. 'Go and enter up your time,' he said sadly. 'If you stick to the tails of the Huns as closely as you stuck to mine, you should make a skyfighter.'

Three days later a little group collected around the notice-board outside the orderly-room.

'What is it?' asked Biggles, trying to reach the board.

'Posting,' said somebody.

Biggles pushed his way to the front and ran his eyes down the alphabetical list of names until he reached his own, and read:

2nd Lieut. Bigglesworth, J., to No. 4 School of Fighting, Frensham.

The posting was dated to take effect from the following day.

He spent the evening hurriedly packing his kit, and, in company with three or four other officers who had been posted to the same aerodrome, caught the night train for his new station.

It was daylight the following day when they arrived, for although the journey to the School of Fighting, which was situated on the Lincolnshire coast, was not a long one, it involved many changes and delays. A tender met them at the station and dropped them with their kits in front of the orderly-room.

Biggles knocked at the door, entered, and saluted.

'Second-Lieutenant Bigglesworth reporting for duty, sir,' he said smartly.

The adjutant consulted a list. 'The mess secretary will fix you up with quarters, Bigglesworth,' he said. 'Get yourself settled as soon as you can and report to "A" Flight—Major Maccleston.' He nodded, and then went on with his work.

Biggles dumped his kit in the room allotted to him, and then made his way to the sheds, where he was told that Major Maccleston was in the air.

He was not surprised, for the air was full of machines— Avros, B.E.s, F.E.s, Pups, and one or two types he did not recognize. Most of them were circling at the far side of the aerodrome and diving at something on the ground. The distant rattle of machine-guns came to his ears.

Later on he learned that the far side of the aerodrome ran straight down into the sea, a long, deserted foreshore, on which old obsolete aeroplanes were placed as targets. Scores of officers stood on the tarmac, singly or in little groups, waiting for their turns to fly.

A Pup taxied out to take off, and he watched it with intense interest, for it was the type that he ultimately hoped to fly. An F.E. was just coming in to land, and he stiffened with horror, knowing that a collision was inevitable.

He saw the gunner in the front seat of the F.E. spring up and cover his face with his arms; then the Pup bored into it from underneath with a dreadful crash of splintering woodwork. For a moment the machines clung together,

21

motionless in mid air; then they broke apart, each spinning into the ground with a terrible noise which, once heard, is never forgotten. A streak of fire ran along the side of one of them, and then a sheet of flame leapt high into the air. An ambulance raced towards the scene, and Biggles turned away, feeling suddenly sick. It was the first real crash he had seen.

A flight-sergeant was watching him grimly. 'A nasty one, sir,' he said casually, as if he had been watching a football match in which one of the players had fallen. 'You'll soon get used to that, though,' he went on, noting Biggles's pale face. 'We killed seven here last week.'

Biggles turned away. Flying no longer seemed just a thrilling game; tragedy stalked it too closely. He was glad when an instructor landed, turned out his passenger, and beckoned him to take his place. Biggles took his seat in the cockpit, noting with a thrill that it was fitted with machine-guns.

'We're going to do a little gunnery practice,' said the instructor, and took off.

Three days later, Biggles was called to the orderly-room.

'What's up?' he asked a sober-faced officer, who was just leaving.

'Heavy casualties in France,' was the reply. 'They're shoving everybody out as fast as they can.'

Biggles entered and saluted. The adjutant handed him a movement order and a railway warrant.

'A tender will leave the mess at six forty-five to catch the seven o'clock train,' he said. 'You will proceed direct to France via Newhaven and Dieppe.'

'But I haven't finished my tests yet, sir!' exclaimed Biggles in surprise.

'Have you got your logbook and training transfer-card?' Biggles placed them on the desk.

The adjutant filled in the tests which had not been marked up, signed them, and then applied the orderly-room stamp.

'You've passed them now,' he said, with a queer smile. 'You may put up your "wings"!'

Biggles saluted, and returned to the aerodrome in a state of suppressed excitement. Two thoughts filled his mind. One was that he was now a fully fledged pilot, entitled to wear the coveted 'wings', and the other that he was going to France.

The fact that he had done less than fifteen hours' flying, dual and solo, did not depress him in the least.

The Boat for France

THERE ARE SOME PEOPLE who say that the North Pole is the most desolate spot on the face of the globe. Others give the doubtful credit to the middle of the Sahara Desert. They are all wrong.

Without the slightest shadow of doubt the most dismal spot on the face of the earth is that depressing railway terminus known as Newhaven Quay, on the south coast of England, where the passenger for the Continent gets out of a train, walks across a platform, and steps on to the cross-Channel boat. At normal times it is bad enough, but during the First World War it was hard to find words to describe it.

So thought Biggles, who crouched rather than sat on a kit-bag in a corner of the platform. His attitude dripped depression as plainly as the dark silhouette of the station dripped moisture.

He was not alone on the platform. At intervals along the stone slabs, dark, ghostly figures loomed mysteriously, in ones and twos, and in little groups. At the far end, a long line of men in greatcoats, with unwieldly-looking bundles on their back, filed slowly into view from an indistinguishable background. The only sounds were vague, muffled orders, and the weird moaning of the biting north-east wind through the rigging of a ship that rested like a great vague shadow against the quay. Not a light showed anywhere, for German submarines had been reported in the Channel. Once, a low laugh echoed eerily from the shadows, and the unusual sound caused those who heard it to turn curiously in the direction whence it came, for he occasion of the departure of a leave-boat for France was not usually one for mirth.

Biggles moved uneasily and seemed to sink a little lower into the greatcoat that enveloped him. He did not even move when another isolated figure emerged slowly from the pillar behind which it had been sheltering from the icy blast, and stopped close by.

'Miserable business, this messing about doing nothing,' observed the newcomer. His voice sounded almost cheerful, and it may have been this quality that caused Biggles to look up.

'Miserable, did you say?' he exclaimed bitterly. 'It's awful. There isn't a word bad enough for it. I'm no longer alive—I'm just a chunk of frozen misery.'

'They say we shall be moving off presently.'

'I've been hearing that ever since I arrived!'

'They say it's a U-boat in the Channel that's holding us up.'

'What about it? Surely to goodness it's better to drown quickly than sit here and freeze to death slowly. Why the dickens don't they let us go on board, anyway?'

'Ask me something easier. Is this your first time over?'

Biggles nodded. 'Yes,' he said grimly, 'and if it's always like this, I hope it will be the last.'

'It probably will be, so you needn't worry about that.'

'What a nice cheerful fellow you are!'

The other laughed softly. 'I see you're R.F.C. What squadron are you going to?'

'I've no idea. My Movement Order takes me as far as the Pool at St. Omer.'

'Splendid! We shall go that far together: I'm in Two-six-six.'

Biggles glanced up with fresh interest. 'So you've been over before?' he queried.

'Had six months of it; just going back from my first leave. By the way, my name's Mahoney—we may as well know each other.'

'Mine's Bigglesworth, though most people find that rather a mouthful and leave off the 'worth.' You fly Pups in Two-six-six, don't you?'

'We do—they're nice little Hun-getters.'

'I hope to goodness I get to a scout squadron, although I haven't flown a scout yet.'

'So much the better,' laughed Mahoney. 'If you'd been flying scouts they'd be certain to put you on bombers when you got to France. Fellows who have been flying two-seaters are usually pitched into scout squadrons. That's the sort of daft thing they do, and one of the reasons why we haven't won the war yet. Hallo! It looks as if we're going to move at last.'

A gangway slid from the quay to the ship with a dull rattle, and the groups of officers and other ranks began to converge upon it.

'Come on, laddie; on your feet and let's get aboard,' continued Mahoney. 'Where's the rest of your kit?'

'Goodness knows! The last I saw of it, it was being slung on to a pile with about a thousand others.'

'Don't worry. It will find you all right. How much flying have you done?'

'Fifteen hours.'

Mahoney shook his head. 'Not enough,' he said. 'Never mind, if you get to Two-six-six, I'll give you a tip or two.'

'You can give me them on the journey, in case I don't,' suggested Biggles. 'I've been waiting for a chance to learn a few things first-hand from someone who has done it.'

'If more chaps would take that view there would be fewer casualties,' said Mahoney soberly, as they crossed over the narrow gangway.

Two days later a Crossley tender pulled up on a lonely, poplar-lined road to the north of St. Omer, and Biggles stepped out. There was nothing in sight to break the bleak inhospitality of the landscape except three many-hued canvas hangars, a cluster of wooden huts, and three or four curious semi-circular corrugated iron buildings.

'Well, here you are, Biggles,' said Mahoney, who had remained inside the vehicle. 'We say good-bye here.'

'So this is One-six-nine Squadron,' replied Biggles, looking about him. 'My word! I must say it doesn't look the sort of place you'd choose for a summer holiday!'

'It isn't. But then you're not on a holiday!' smiled

26

Mahoney. 'Don't worry; you'll find things cheerful enough inside. It's too bad they wouldn't let you go to a scout squadron; but F.E.s aren't so bad. They can fight when they have to, and the Huns know it, believe me. I suppose they're so short of pilots that they are just bunging fellows straight to the squadrons where pilots are most needed. Well, I must get along; Two-six-six is only seven or eight miles farther on, so we shall be seeing something of each other. Come over to our next guest night. Remember what I've told you—and you may live until next Christmas. Cheerio, laddie!'

'Cheerio!' replied Biggles, with a wave of farewell as the car sped on to its destination. He picked up his valise and walked towards a square wooden building near the hangars, which he rightly judged to be the squadron office. He tapped on the door, opened it in response to a curt invitation to enter, and saluted briskly.

'Second-Lieutenant Bigglesworth, sir,' he said.

An officer who sat at a desk strewn with papers, rose, came towards him, and offered his hand. 'Pleased to meet you, Bigglesworth,' he said. 'And if you can fly, everyone here will be more than pleased to see you. We are having a tough time just at present. I'm Todd—more often known as "Toddy"—and I'm simply the Recording Officer. The C.O. is in the air, but he'll want a word with you when he gets back. You'll like Major Paynter. Wing 'phoned us that you were on the way, so you'll find your quarters ready in Number Four Hut. Get your kit inside, and make yourself comfortable; then go across to the mess. I'll be along presently. By the way, how many hours' flying—solo—have you done?'

'Nearly nine hours.'

Toddy grimaced. 'What on?' he asked.

'Shorthorns and Avros.'

'Ever flown an F.E.?'

'Not solo. I had a flight in one at Frensham, but an instructor was in the other seat.'

'Never mind; they're easy enough to fly,' answered Toddy. 'See you later.'

Biggles departed to his quarters. The work of unpacking his kit occupied only a few minutes, and then he made his way slowly towards the officers' mess. He was still a little distance away, when the sound of an aero-engine made him glance upwards. An aeroplane was heading towards the aerodrome, a type which he did not recognize. But, unwilling to betray his ignorance before possible spectators in the mess, he paid no further attention to it and continued on his course. He then noted with some surprise that Toddy was behaving in a very odd manner. The Recording Officer began by flinging open the door of the squadron office and racing towards the mess. When he had reached about half-way, however, he appeared to change his mind, and, turning like a hare, took a flying leap into a sort of hole.

Biggles next noticed the faces of several officers at the mess window; they seemed to be very excited about something, waving their arms wildly. It did not occur to him for a moment that the signals were intended for him. The first indication he received that something unusual was happening was a curious whistling sound; but even then the full significance of it did not strike him. The whistle swiftly became a shrill howl, and thinking he was about to be run down by a speedy car, he jumped sideways. The movement probably saved his life, for the next instant the world seemed to explode around him in a brilliant flash of flame. There was a thundering detonation that seemed to make the very earth rock, and he was flung violently to the ground. For a moment he lay quite still, dazed, while a steady downpour of clods, stones, and loose earth rained about him.

The steady rattle of machine-guns in action penetrated his temporarily paralysed brain, and he rose unsteadily to his feet. He noted that the aeroplane had disappeared, and that a little crowd of officers and mechanics were racing towards him.

'What the dickens was that?' he asked the officers who ran up.

The question seemed to amuse them, for a yell of laughter rose into the air.

Biggles flushed. 'Do you usually greet new fellows like that?' he inquired angrily.

There was a renewed burst of laughter.

'Jerry does, when he gets the chance. Our friends over the Line must have heard that you had just arrived, so they sent their love and kisses,' replied a tall, good-looking officer, with a wink at the others. 'Don't you know an L.V.G. when you see one?' he added.

'An L.V.G.! A Hun!' cried Biggles.

The others nodded. 'Yes. Just slipped over to lay the daily egg. You're lucky,' he went on. 'When I saw you strolling across the aerodrome as if you were taking an airing in the park, I thought we should be packing up your kit by this time. You're Bigglesworth, I suppose; we heard you were coming. My name is Mapleton, of A Flight. This is Marriot—Lutters—Way—McAngus. We're all A Flight. The others are in the air. But come across to the mess and make yourself at home!'

'But what about that L.V.G.?' cried Biggles. 'Do you let him get away with that sort of thing?'

'He's half-way home by now; the best thing we can hope for is that the Line archies give him a warm time. Hallo, here comes the patrol! What——'

A sudden hush fell upon the group as all eyes turned upwards to where two machines were coming in to land. Biggles noticed that Mapleton's face had turned oddly pale and strained. He noticed, too, for the first time, that there were three stars on his sleeves, which indicated the rank of captain.

'Two!' breathed the man whom Captain Mapleton had named Marriot. 'Two!' he said again. And Biggles could feel a sudden tension in the air.

'Come on!' said Mapleton. 'Let's go and meet them. Maybe the others have stayed on a bit longer.'

Together they hurried towards the now taxi-ing machines.

The events of the next few minutes were to live in Biggles' mind for ever. His whole system, brought face to face with the grim realities of war, received a shock which sent his nerves leaping like a piece of taut elastic that has been severed with scissors. He was hardly conscious of it

29

at the time, however, when, with the others, he reached the leading machine. He merely looked at it curiously. Then, instinctively, he looked at the pilot, who was pushing up his goggles very slowly and deliberately.

One glance at his face and Biggles knew he was in the presence of tragedy. The face was drawn and white, but it was the expression on it—or, rather, the absence of expression on it—that made Biggles catch his breath. There was no fear written there, but rather a look of weariness. For perhaps two minutes he sat thus, staring with unseeing eyes at his instrument-board. Then, with a movement that was obviously an effort, he passed his hand wearily over his face and climbed stiffly to the ground. Still without speaking he began to walk towards the mess, followed by two or three of the officers.

A low, muttered exclamation made Biggles half-turn to the man next to him. It was Lutters.

'Just look at that kite!' Lutters said. 'The Old Man must have been through hell backwards.'

'Old Man?' ejaculated Biggles questioningly.

'Yes—the C.O. There must be two hundred bullet holes in that machine; how it holds together beats me!'

Biggles' attention had been so taken up with the pilot that he had failed to notice the machine, and now he caught his breath as he looked at it. There were holes everywhere; in several places pieces of torn canvas hung loosely, having been wrenched into long, narrow streamers by the wind. One of the interplane struts was splintered for more than half its length, and a flying wire trailed uselessly across the lower 'plane.

He was about to take a step nearer, when a cry made him look towards the second machine. Two mechanics were carefully lifting a limp body to the ground.

'You'd better keep out of the way,' said McAngus brusquely, as he passed; but Biggles paid no attention. He knew that McAngus was right, and that the sight was hardly one for a new pilot; but the tableau drew him irresistibly towards it.

When he reached the machine they had laid the mortally wounded pilot on the ground. His eyes were open, but there was an expression in them that Biggles had never seen before.

'Jimmy—how's Jimmy?' the stricken man was muttering; and then: 'Look after Jimmy!'

Biggles felt himself roughly pushed aside.

It was the C.O., who had returned. 'Get him to hospital as fast as you can,' he told the driver of the motor-ambulance which had pulled up alongside. Then, 'How's Mr. Forrester?' he asked a mechanic, who was bending over the front cockpit of the machine.

'I'm afraid he's dead, sir,' was the quiet reply.

'All right—get him out!' said the C.O. briefly.

Biggles watched two mechanics swing up to the forward cockpit of the F.E. Slowly, and with great care, they lifted the body of the dead observer and lowered it into waiting hands below.

Biggles caught a glimpse of a pale, waxen face, wearing a curious, fixed smile, and then he turned away, feeling that he was in the middle of a ghastly dream, from which he would presently awaken. He was overwhelmed with a sense of fantastic unreality.

Again the drone of an aero-engine rose and fell on the breeze, and at the same instant a voice cried: 'Here's another!' He swung round and stood expectant with the others as the machine reached the aerodrome, roared low over their heads as it came round into the wind, and then landed. A large white letter U was painted on the nose.

'It's Allen and Thompson!' cried several at once.

The machine taxied up quickly. The observer leaped out as soon as it stopped, and started buffing his arms to restore the circulation. The pilot joined him on the ground, flung open his flying-coat and lit a cigarette.

Biggles saw there were several bullet-holes in this machine, too, but neither pilot nor observer paid any attention to them. In fact, the pilot, a stockily built, red-faced youth, was grinning cheerfully, and Biggles stared in amazement at a man who could laugh in the shadow of death.

'Love old Ireland!' observed Thompson, the observer. 'Isn't it perishing cold! Give me a match, somebody. What a day!' he went on. 'The sky's fairly raining Huns. The

31

old man got a couple—did he tell you? Poor Jimmy's gone, I'm afraid, and Lucas. We ran into the biggest bunch of Huns over Douai that I ever saw in my life.'

He turned and walked away towards the mess, the others following, and Biggles was left alone with the mechanics, who were now pulling the machines into the hangars with excited comments on the damage they had suffered. He watched them for a few minutes, and then, deep in thought, followed the other officers towards the mess, feeling strangely subdued. For the first time he had looked upon death, and although he was not afraid, something inside him seemed to have changed. Hitherto he had regarded the War as 'fun'. But he now perceived that he had been mistaken. It was one thing to read of death in the newspapers, but quite another matter to see it in reality.

Several officers were in the room when Biggles entered, and he felt rather self-conscious of his inexperience; but the C.O. soon put him at ease.

'I'm afraid you've come at rather a bad moment,' he began, shaking hands. 'I mean for yourself,' he added quickly. 'We hope it will be a good one for us. I'm posting you to A Flight; Captain Mapleton will be your flight-commander. We like to keep pilots and observers together, as far as we can, but it's not always possible. I believe Way is without a regular pilot, isn't he, Mapleton? So Bigglesworth might pair off with him.'

Captain Mapleton nodded. 'Yes, sir,' he said. 'He's my only observer now without a regular pilot.'

'Good! Then your Flight is now up to establishment,' continued the major, turning again to Biggles. 'Don't let what you've seen to-day depress you. It was an unfortunate moment for you to arrive; that sort of thing doesn't happen every day, thank goodness!' He hesitated and went on, 'I want you always to remember that the honour of the squadron comes first. We are going through rather a difficult time just now, and we may have a lot of uphill work ahead of us, so we're all doing our best. Trust your flight-commander implicitly, and always follow his instructions. In the ordinary way I should give you a week or two to

32

get your bearings before letting you go over the Line, but we've had a bad run of casualties, and I need every officer I can get hold of. It's rather bad luck on you, but I want you to do the best you can in the circumstances. Study the map and the photographs in the map-room; in that way you will soon become acquainted with the area. All right, gentlemen, that's all.'

As the officers filed out, a deeply tanned, keen-eyed young officer tapped Biggles on the arm. 'I'm Mark Way,' he said. 'It looks as if we shall be flying together, so the sooner we know each other the better.'

'That's true,' said Biggles. 'Have you been out here long?'

'Nearly three months,' replied Mark simply. 'But I saw a bit of active service with the infantry before I transferred to the R.F.C. I came over with the New Zealand contingent; my home is out there.'

'Sporting of you to come all this way to help us. Who have you been flying with?'

'Lane.'

'Where is he now?'

Mark gave Biggles a sidelong glance. 'He's gone topsides,' he said slowly. 'He died in hospital last week—bullet through the lungs.'

Biggles was silent for a moment, feeling rather embarrassed.

'You'll like Mapleton,' went on Mark. 'He's a good sort. By the way, we call him Mabs; I don't know why, but he was called that when I came here. Marble is his observer—his real name is Mardell, but Marble is a good name for him. He's as cold as ice in a dog-fight, and knows every inch of the Line. They're a jolly good pair, and I'd follow them anywhere. Allen is O.C. B Flight. It's best to keep out of his way; he's a bad-tempered brute. Perhaps it isn't quite fair of me to say that, because I don't think he means to be nasty; he's been out here a long time, and his nerves are all to pieces. Rayner has C Flight. He's all right, but a bit of a snob, although personally I think it's all affectation. His brother was killed early in the war, and all he really thinks about is revenge. He's got several Huns. He

33

takes on Huns wherever he finds them, regardless of numbers, and he gets his Flight into pretty hot water; but they can't complain, because he's always in the thick of it himself. I don't think his luck can last much longer. I wouldn't be his observer for anything! Marriot and Mc-Angus are the other two pilots in A Flight. Conway flies with Marriot, and Lutter is Mac's observer; they're a good crowd. Hallo, here comes Mabs. What does he want?'

'Bigglesworth,' began the flight-commander, coming up, 'I don't want to rush you, but I'm taking a Line patrol up this evening. I think it will be pretty quiet, or I wouldn't let you come, even if you wanted to. But the fact is, everybody has been flying all hours, and it will mean extra flying if someone has to make a special journey to show you the Lines. And it isn't as if we were flying single-seaters; you've always got Mark with you to put you right if you get adrift. So if you care to come this evening it will serve two purposes. You'll get a squint at the Line and a whiff of archie, and it will give McAngus a rest. He's looking a bit knocked up.'

'Certainly I'll come,' replied Biggles quickly.

'That's fine! I thought you wouldn't mind. It's all for your own good, in the long run, because the sooner you get used to archie the better. But for goodness' sake keep close to me. You keep your eye on him, Mark. We take off at three o'clock, but be on the tarmac a quarter of an hour before that, and I'll show you our proposed course while the engines are warming up.'

Battle

IT WAS UNDER A COLD, grey sky, that Biggles sat in his cockpit the same afternoon, waiting for the signal to take off. He had made one short flight over the aerodrome immediately after lunch to accustom himself to his new machine, and he had satisfied himself that he was able to fly it without difficulty. The F.E.2b. was not a difficult machine to fly; it had no vicious habits, which was, perhaps, the reason why those who flew it were unstinted in their praise.

The patrol was made up of three machines. Captain Mapleton, of course, was leading. Marriot and his gunner, 'Con' Conway, were on the right, and Biggles, with Mark Way in the front seat, on the left.

The machine was fitted with two machine-guns, one firing forward and the other backwards over the top 'plane, both operated by the gunner. A rack containing drums of ammunition was fitted to the inside of the cockpit.

Biggles felt a thrill of excitement run through him as the flight-commander's machine began to move forward; he heard Marriot's engine roar, and then the sound was drowned in the bellow of his own as he opened the throttle. Together the three machines tore across the damp aerodrome and then soared into the air, turning slowly in a wide circle.

A quarter of an hour later they were still over the aerodrome, but at a height of seven thousand feet, and Biggles, who had settled down into the long turn, dashed off at a tangent as the leader suddenly straightened out and headed towards the east. A sharp exclamation from the watchful Mark warned him of his error, which he hastened to rectify.

although he still remained at a little distance from the other machines.

'Try to keep up!' yelled Mark, turning in his seat and smiling encouragingly. 'It's easier for everybody then.'

Biggles put his nose down a little to gain extra speed, and then zoomed back into position, a manœuvre which Mark acknowledged with an approving wave. For some time they flew on without incident, and then Mark began to move about in his cockpit, looking towards every point of the compass in turn, and searching the sky above and the earth below with long, penetrating stares.

Once he reached for his gun, and caused Biggles' heart to jump by firing a short burst downwards. But then Biggles remembered that Mark had said he would fire a burst when they reached the Line, to warm the guns, which would reduce the chance of a jam.

Following the line of the gun-barrel, he looked down and saw an expanse of brown earth, perhaps a mile in width, merging gradually into dull green on either side. Tiny zig-zag lines ran in all directions. Must be the Lines, he thought, with a quiver of excitement, not unmixed with apprehension, and he continued to look down with interest and awe.

'Hi!'

He looked up with a guilty start; Mark was yelling at him, and he saw the reason—he had drifted a good hundred yards from his companions.

'My hat!' he mused. 'I shall never see anything if I can't take my eyes off them without losing them.'

But Mark was pointing with outstretched finger over the side of the cockpit, and, following the line indicated, he saw a little group of round, black blobs floating in space. Automatically he counted them; there were five—no, six. He blinked and looked again. There were eight. 'That's queer!' he muttered, and even as the truth dawned upon him there was a flash of flame near his wing-tip, and a dull explosion that could be heard above the noise of the engine.

The swerve of the machine brought his heart into his mouth, but he righted it quickly and looked around for the other two. They had disappeared. For a moment he nearly

36

panicked, but Mark's casual nod in the direction of his right wing restored his confidence, and, peering forward, he perceived them about fifty yards or so to his right. He turned quickly into his proper place, receiving a nod of approval from his gunner as he did so.

The black archie bursts were all around them now, but Mark did not appear to notice them; he had reached for his gun and held it in a position of readiness. Suddenly he dragged it to the other side and fired again.

Biggles nearly strained his neck trying to see what Mark was shooting at, but seeing nothing but empty air decided that he must be warming up his guns again. He looked across at the machine on his right, and noticed that Conway was shooting, too. As he watched him he ceased firing and looked down over the side of his cockpit for a long time; then he looked across at Mark and held up his fist, thumb pointing upwards.

'There seems to be a lot of signalling going on!' thought Biggles. 'I wonder what it's all about?'

The time passed slowly, and he began to feel bored and rather tired, for it was the longest flight he had ever made. This seems a pretty tame business, he pondered. I should have liked to see a Hun or two, just to get an idea of what they looked like. 'Hallo!'

Mark was standing up again, trying to point his gun straight down, and for the first time he seemed to be excited. Casually Biggles leaned over the side to see what it was that could interest his gunner to such an extent. There, immediately below him, not fifty yards away, was a large green swept-back wing, but that which held his gaze and caused his lips to part in horrified amazement were the two enormous black Maltese crosses, one on each end. His skin turned to goose flesh and his lips went dry. He saw a man standing in the back seat of the machine pointing something at him; then, for no reason that he could discover, the man fell limply sideways, and the green wing folded up like a piece of tissue paper. It turned over on its side and the man fell out.

In a kind of paralysed fascination Biggles watched the

37

brown, leather-clad body turning slowly over and over as it fell. He thought it would never reach the ground.

He was brought to his senses with a jerk by a shrill yell. The other two machines were turning—had nearly completed the turn. He swung round after them in a frantic bank, skidding in a manner that made Mark clutch at the side of his cockpit. He could see no other German machines in sight, so he decided that the time allotted for their patrol had expired.

'My word, now he has decided to go home, he is certainly going in a hurry!' thought Biggles, as the leading machine nearly stood on its nose as it dived full out towards the ground. He thrust his joy-stick forward, and with difficulty restrained a yell of delight.

The shriek of the propeller, the howl of the wind in the wires, seemed to get into his blood and intoxicate him. He wondered vaguely why Mark was looking back over his shoulder instead of looking where they were going and enjoying the fun, and he was almost sorry when the flight-commander pulled out of the dive and commenced to glide down.

He watched the ground closely, noting such landmarks as he thought he would be able to recognize again, until the aerodrome came into view, when he concentrated on the business of landing.

A green Very light soared upwards from the leading machine, and then dropped swiftly; it was the 'wash-out' signal, meaning that the machines were to land independently. He allowed the others to land first, and then, with exultation in his heart, he followed them down and taxied up to the hangars.

Mark gave him a queer smile as he switched off the engine. 'Pretty good!' he said cheerfully. 'That's one on the slate for me on Lane's account.'

'You mean that green Hun underneath us?' cried Biggles. 'My gosh! It gave me a queer feeling to see that fellow going down.'

'Great Scott, no! Conway got him. I got the blue-and-yellow devil.'

'What!' exclaimed Biggles, in amazement. 'What blue-and-yellow devil?'

'Didn't you see him diving down on us from in front? He was after you.'

'No, I didn't, and that's a fact,' admitted Biggles soberly. 'I didn't see you shoot at him.'

'I couldn't at first, because I was busy plastering the black fellow who was peppering us from underneath.'

Biggles blinked and shook his head. 'Black, blue, green! How the dickens many of them were there?' he muttered, in a dazed voice.

'Seven altogether. We got three of them between us.'

Biggles sat down limply. 'And I only saw one!' he groaned. 'What on earth would have happened to me if I'd been alone?'

Mark laughed. 'Don't worry, you'll soon get the hang of spotting 'em,' he said. 'You saw that mob coming down on us at the finish?'

Biggles shook his head, eyes wide open. He couldn't speak.

'You didn't? You ought to have seen those—there must have been more than a dozen of 'em. Mabs spotted them the instant they shoved their ugly noses out of the mist, and like a sensible fellow he streaked for home.'

'Thank goodness he did!' muttered Biggles weakly. 'And I thought he was merely hurrying home!'

'That's just what he was doing,' observed Mark dryly. 'But let's go and get some tea—I can do with it!'

Plots and Plans

BIGGLES LANDED his F.E. after a short test flight and glanced in the direction of the sheds, where Mabs and the rest of the flight were standing watching him.

A week had elapsed since his first never-to-be-forgotten flight over the Lines. He had done at least one patrol every day since, and was already beginning to feel that he was an old hand at the game. He had picked up the art of war flying with an aptitude that had amazed everyone, particularly his flight-commander, who had reported to Major Paynter, the C.O., that young Biggles seemed to have a sort of second sight where enemy aircraft were concerned.

He jumped down now from the cockpit and with a brief 'She's running nicely!' to his fitter, walked quickly towards the flight shed, where the others were apparently waiting for him.

'Come on!' announced Mabs, with a curious smile. 'There's a little party on, and we knew you wouldn't like to be left out.'

'You're right!' agreed Biggles. 'What's it about? I like parties.'

'You may not like this one,' said Mabs. 'Stand fast while I get it off my chest. You know, of course, that headquarters have been shouting for days about a report they want making on the railway junction and sidings at Vanfleur?'

'You mean the show that Littleton and Gormsby went on?'

'That's right. As you know, they didn't come back. Neither did Blake nor Anderson, who went yesterday. Both the other flights have had a shot at it, and now it's our

40

turn. The Old Man says I'm not to go, otherwise I shouldn't be here telling you about it. That means that either you or Marriot or McAngus will have to go.'

'I'd already worked that out,' replied Biggles. 'Nothing wrong with that, is there?'

'Nothing! I'm just telling you, that's all. You can settle amongst yourselves who's going, or if there's any argument about it I shall have to detail someone for the job. I'm not going to ask for volunteers, because you'd all volunteer on principle, and nothing would be decided. But there's two things you've got to remember. In the first place, it's no use going all the way to Vanfleur and coming back without learning something. It means counting every wagon and truck in the siding, and noting any dumps in the vicinity. In other words, the information has got to be correct. It's no use guessing or imagining things, because incorrect information is misleading, and does more harm than good. The other thing is, it's going to be a tricky show for the man who goes. Vanfleur is forty miles over the Line, if it's an inch. You don't need me to tell you that there are more Hun scouts at Douai than any Boche aerodrome on the front. Rumour says that Richthofen and his crowd have just moved to Douai, and maybe that's why the other fellows didn't get back. Well, there it is. Tell me in five minutes who's going.'

'I'll go!' said Biggles promptly.

'No, you don't!' replied Mabs quickly. 'I'm not letting anyone commit suicide just because he thinks it's the right thing to do. I suggest you toss for it—odd man goes—that's the fairest way, and then whatever happens there can be no reproaches about it.'

Biggles took a coin from his pocket and the others did the same. 'Spin,' he said, and tossed the coin into the air. The three coins rang on the concrete.

'Heads,' said Biggles, looking at his own coin.

'Tails,'' announced Marriot.

'Same here,' said McAngus

'That means I'm the boob!' grinned Biggles. 'When do I start?'

'When you like—the sooner the better. I should think

first thing in the morning might be the best time,' suggested Mabs.

'Why do you think that?'

'Well, that's the time these shows are usually done.'

'That's what I thought—and the Huns know that as well as we do. I'll go this afternoon, just by way of a change, if it's all the same to you. What do you think, Mark?'

'Suits me!'

'That's that, then!' said Mabs. 'You'd better come with me and tell the Old Man you're going. He'll want to have a word with you first. And you'd better come along, too, Mark.'

The C.O. looked up from his desk when they entered the squadron office. 'Ah, so it's you, Bigglesworth, and Way. I had an idea it might be.' He rose to his feet and walked over to them. 'Now look here, you fellows,' he went. 'There isn't much I can say, but remember that these shows are not carried out just for the fun of it, or to find us jobs of work. They are of the greatest possible importance to H.Q., as they themselves are beginning to admit.' He smiled whimsically, recalling the days when the military leaders had laughed at the idea of aeroplanes being of practical value for reconnoitring. 'I want you to pay particular attention to the rolling stock in the sidings,' he resumed. 'Also, have a good look at these places I've marked on the map. Study the last set of photographs we got of the area—you'll find them in the map-room. You know what to look out for; make a note of any alterations in the landscape.

'If you see a clump of bushes growing where there were none last week, when the photos were taken, it probably means that it is a camouflaged battery. Watch for "blazes" on the grass, caused by the flash of the guns, and cables leading to the spot. You will not be able to see telephone wires, of course, but you may see the shadows cast by the poles, or a row of dots—the newly turned earth at the foot of each pole. You may see a track joining the dots—the footmarks and beaten-down grass caused by the working party. It's easier still to pick out an underground cable. If the trench has not been filled in, it shows as a clear-cut line; if it has been filled in, it reveals itself as a sort of woolly line, blurred at the edges. If you see several such lines of communication converging on one spot it may mean that there is an enemy headquarters there.

'Quantities of fresh barbed wire means that the enemy is expecting to be attacked, and has prepared new positions upon which to retire. On the other hand, new trenches, saps, dug-outs, and, more particularly, light railways, means that he is preparing an offensive. But there, you should have learned about these things by now so there's no need for me to go over them again. When have you decided to go?'

'After lunch, sir,' replied Biggles.

'I thought you'd start in the morning: that's the usual time.'

'Yes, sir; that's why we decided to go this afternoon.'

The C.O. frowned, then a smile spread over his face. 'Good for you!' he said, nodding approval. 'That's the worst of being out here a long time; we get into habits without knowing it. Little points like the one you've just mentioned have been staring us in the face so long that we can't see them. All right, then. Good luck!'

'Come on, Mark!' said Biggles, when they had left the office. 'Let's get the machine ready. Then we can sit back and think things over until it's time to go.'

It was exactly two o'clock when they took off. The distance to their objective was, Mabs had said, a full forty miles, and as they expected to be away at least three hours, they dared not start later, as it began to get dark soon after four.

For twenty minutes Biggles climbed steeply, crossing and recrossing the aerodrome as he bored his way upwards, knowing that the higher they were when they crossed the Lines the less chance there would be of being molested; so he waited until the altimeter was nearly on the eight thousand feet mark before striking out for the Lines.

A few desultory archie bursts greeted them as they passed over, and for the next half-hour they had the sky to themselves. It was a good day for their purpose from one point of view, but a bad day from another aspect.

Great masses of wet clouds were drifting sluggishly eastward at various altitudes—6,000, 8,000 and even at 10,000 feet—and while this might afford cover in the event of their being attacked, it also provided cover for prowling enemy scouts to lie in wait for them. Again, while it concealed them from the gunners on the ground, it limited their range of vision and prevented them from seeing many of the landmarks they had decided to follow. Moreover, if their objective was concealed by cloud, they would either have to return with their mission unfulfilled, or they would have to descend very low, a dangerous performance so far over enemy territory. Nevertheless, Biggles had decided that unless enemy interference made the project hopeless, he would go down to a thousand feet, if necessary, rather than return with a blank report, which, rightly or wrongly, would be regarded as failure by headquarters.

They were now approaching the objective, and Biggles began to hope that they might achieve their object without firing a single shot. But the atmosphere rapidly thickened, and he realized with annoyance that a blanket of mist hung over the very spot they had come so far and risked so much to view. He shut off his engine and began a gentle glide.

'I'm going down!' he roared to Mark, who stood up in his seat, guns ready for action, scanning the atmosphere anxiously in all directions.

At six thousand feet they sank into the billowing mist, and Biggles turned his eyes to his instruments, every nerve tense. 5,000—4,000—3,000 feet, and still there was no break, and he knew he would never be able to climb up through it again without losing control of the machine. He hoped desperately that he would find a hole, or at least a thin patch, in the cloud, after their work was accomplished. At two thousand feet he emerged into a cold, cheerless world, and looked about anxiously for the railway line. 'There it is!' he yelled, pointing to the right, at the same time opening up his engine and heading towards it. Mark had seen the junction at the same instant, and, leaving his guns, grabbed his note-book and prepared to write.

Whoof, whoof, whoof, barked the archie; but the enemy gunners were shooting hurriedly, and the shots went wide. Other guns joined in, and the bursts began to come closer

44

as the gunners corrected their aim. But Biggles kept the machine on even keel as he watched the sky around them, while Mark counted the railway trucks, jotting down his notes as well as his cold hands and the sometimes swaying machine would permit.

Biggles made a complete circuit around the railway junction, which was as choc-a-bloc with traffic as only a railway junction of strategical importance could be in time of war.

Four long trains were in the station itself; two others—one consisting of open trucks, carrying field artillery—stood in a siding, with steam up and ready to move. Shells were being loaded in the other from a great dump.

'Have you finished?' yelled Biggles.

'Go round once more!' bellowed Mark.

Biggles frowned, but proceeded to make another circuit, twisting and turning from time to time to dodge the ever-increasing archie and machine-gun bullets. Wish I had a bomb or two, he thought, as he eyed the great ammunition dump. But there, no doubt the bombers will arrive in due course, when we've made our report.

Without warning the archie stopped abruptly. Mark dropped his pencil, shoved his writing-pad into his pocket, and grabbed his gun. 'Look out!' he yelled.

But Biggles had already seen them—a big formation of straight-winged planes sweeping up from the east. There was no need to speculate as to their nationality.

'What a mob!' he muttered, and swung round for home. But an icy hand clutched his heart as he beheld yet another formation of enemy machines racing towards the spot from the direction of the Lines. They were cut off.

We stayed too long, he thought bitterly. The people at the station must have rung up every squadron for miles, and they're not going to let us get our report home if they can prevent it. 'Well, I can't fight that lot!' he muttered desperately, and, turning his nose to the north-west, raced away in the only direction open to him.

Fortunately there was a lot of broken cloud on the horizon, apart from a big mass overhead, and this, he hoped, would help him to throw the wolves off his trail.

45

Mark suddenly crouched low behind the gun that fired backwards over the top 'plane, and began firing in short, sharp bursts. Biggles winced as a bullet bored through his instrument-board with a vicious thud. He began side-slipping gently to and fro to throw the enemy pilots off their mark—a tip that had been given him on the boat coming over. A faint rattle reached his ears above the noise of the engine. They're overtaking us, he thought. Mark signalled frantically to him to climb. He put his nose down for an instant to gather speed, and then zoomed upwards. The cold, grey mist enveloped them like a blanket.

'Must be twenty of 'em—Albatripes!' yelled Mark.

But Biggles was busy fighting to keep the machine on even keel. The bubble of the inclinometer was jumping from one side to the other in a most alarming way, and the needle of his compass was swinging violently. 'It's no use— I'll have to go down!' he yelled. A blast of air struck him on the side of the face and he knew he was side-slipping; he rectified the slip, but, as usual in such cases, he overdid it, and the draught struck his other cheek. He shot out of the cloud with one wing pointing straight to the ground.

He picked the machine up while Mark clambered to his feet, searching the atmosphere behind them. Biggles, snatching a glance behind him, saw enemy machines scattered all over the sky to the south-east, still effectually barring their return. No sooner did the lone F.E. appear than they turned in its direction and began overhauling it.

'I don't know where we're getting, but I can't face that lot,' shouted Biggles, still heading north-west. 'We must be miles off our course.'

The black-crossed machines were closing the gap between them quickly, so he pushed his nose down and raced towards the low clouds, now only a short distance away. He reached them just as a burst of fire from the rear made the F.E. quiver from propeller-boss to tail-skid, and he plunged into the nearest mass of white, woolly vapour in something like a panic. He came out on the other side, banked vertically to the left, and plunged into another.

And so he went on, twisting and turning, sometimes through and sometimes around the clouds. He dived below them and then zoomed up again through them. He knew he was hopelessly lost, but even that, he decided, was better than facing the overwhelming odds against them.

Mark, still standing up, was examining the sky behind them; then he held up his fists, thumbs pointing upwards.

'O.K.! We've lost them!' he bellowed.

Biggles breathed a sigh of relief and began to glide down through the cloud, hoping to pick up some outstanding landmark that might be recognized from his map. The F.E. emerged once more into clear air, and he looked down anxiously. He stared, blinked, and stared again as a dark green expanse of foam-lashed water met his horrified gaze.

There could be no mistake. He was looking down at the sea. The clouds, as so often happens, ended abruptly at the coast-line, which revealed itself as a white, surf-lashed line just behind him. In front of him the sky was a clear, pale blue as far as he could see.

He thought quickly, feeling for his map, guessing what had happened. In their long rush to the north-west they had actually reached the Belgian coast, so he turned to the south, knowing that sooner or later they were bound to reach France again.

Mark, too, examined his map as Biggles began following the coast-line.

'We shall be all right if the petrol holds out, and if it doesn't get dark before we can see where we are,' he shouted, and then settled back in his seat, to resume the eternal task of watching the sky for enemy machines. Slowly the blue of the sky turned to misty grey with the approach of dusk, and Biggles came lower in order not to lose the coast-line.

Suddenly Mark sprang to his feet and swung his gun round to face the open sea. Biggles, following the line of the gun, saw an Albatros diving on them out of the mist. Something, it may have been pure instinct, made him glance in the opposite direction—a second Albatros was coming in on their left, the landward side. Two scouts, evidently working together, were launching a dual attack.

The events of the next thirty seconds followed each other so swiftly that they outraced Biggles' capacity for thinking.

Mark was shooting steadily at the first scout, which had now opened fire on them; Biggles was watching the second, which was also shooting. The pilots of both enemy scouts, evidently old hands at the game, thrust home their attack so closely that Biggles instinctively zoomed to avoid collision; but they both swerved at the last moment in the same direction. They met head-on just below and in front of the F.E. with a crash that made Biggles jump. At the same instant his engine cut out dead, and a pungent, almost overpowering stench of petrol filled his nostrils. Automatically he put his nose down towards the shore. Out of the corner of his eye he saw the fragments of the two German scouts strike the water with a terrific splash.

Late for Dinner

In the now failing light the coast-line, although fairly close, was not much more than a dark, indistinct mass, with a strip of pale orange sand, lashed with white foam, running along the edge.

'We shall never reach it!' thought Biggles, as he glanced at his altimeter. It registered one thousand feet.

Mark was standing up, calmly divesting himself of his leather coat and flying-boots. He tore off the two top pages of his writing-pad and folded the precious report carefully into a leather wallet, which he thrust into his breeches pocket.

He lifted the guns off their mountings and tossed them overboard, and Biggles knew that he did this for two reasons. Firstly, to prevent them falling into the hands of the enemy, and secondly, to lighten the machine, and thus give them a better chance of reaching the shore.

Then Mark looked at Biggles, and, cupping his hands round his mouth, shouted: 'Get your clothes off. It looks as if we shall have to swim for it!'

With some difficulty, first holding the joy-stick with one hand and then the other, Biggles managed to get his coat off and throw it overboard. Cap, goggles and sheepskin flying-boots followed.

At the last moment, just as he thought they might reach the beach, a slant of wind caught them and they dropped swiftly. He held the machine off as long as he could, but as it lost flying speed it wobbled and then flopped bodily into the water. A wave lifted the doomed F.E. like a feather and rushed it towards the beach; then, as it grated harshly on the sand, they jumped clear and struck out for the shore.

Half drowned, Biggles felt a wave roll him over and over. It dropped him on all fours on solid ground, and he dug his fingers into the sand as he felt the backwash sucking him back again. Mark, who was heavier, grabbed him by the collar and clung to him desperately until the wave had receded. Crawling, swaying, stumbling and falling, they managed to reach the beach, gasping and spitting out mouthfuls of sea-water.

'My hat, isn't it cold!' muttered Biggles through chattering teeth.

'Come on, get on your feet—they'll be here any minute. They must have seen us come down!' snapped Mark; and at a reeling gait in their water-logged clothes they hurried towards the wide sand dunes which line that part of the Belgian coast.

'What's the hurry?' panted Biggles.

'The Huns will be here any minute—we're still the wrong side of the Lines!'

Hardly had they plunged into the bewildering valleys of the dunes than they heard the sound of harsh, guttural voices coming towards them.

'Down!' hissed Mark, and they flung themselves flat in the coarse, scrubby grass that grew in patches on the sand. It was now nearly dark, so there was still just a chance that they might escape observation.

Biggles clenched his teeth tightly in order to restrain their chattering, which he thought would betray them, while the voices passed not more than ten yards away and receded in the direction of the shore.

For twenty minutes or more they lay while dark figures loomed around them, going towards or returning from the beach. One party came so close that Biggles held his breath, expecting to feel a heavy boot in the small of his back at any moment.

'What are we going to do? I shall freeze to death if we stay here much longer!' he whispered as the footsteps receded.

'So shall I if it comes to that,' muttered Mark. 'I'm dead from the feet up. But our only chance is to lie still and hope that they'll think we were drowned. They must have seen the two Albatripes attack us, and for all they know we might have been wounded. There are bound to be people on the beach for some time watching for the bodies of those two Boche pilots. We shall have to put up with the cold for a minute or two while people are moving about. When it gets a bit darker we'll crawl to the top of a dune and see if we can see what's going on.'

Another quarter of an hour passed, and at last it was really dark, except for the feeble light of a crescent moon low in the sky. With a whispered 'Come on!' Mark began crawling up the sloping side of the nearest sand dune, and Biggles followed, glad to be moving at last. Side by side they reached the top, and, raising their heads slowly, peered round. Not a soul was in sight except on the beach, where a small group of figures could just be made out watching the remains of the F.E. being pounded to pieces by the surf. Some debris had evidently been salved, for it lay in a pile just beyond the reach of the waves.

'They must think we were drowned or there'd be more activity,' breathed Mark. 'Our only chance now is to work our way along the coast. It might be better if we waited a bit longer, but we can't do that or we shall be frozen to death. Anyway, we've got to be round the wire before morning or we shall certainly be spotted.'

'Wire—what wire?' asked Biggles.

'The barbed wire between the Lines. I'm not absolutely certain but I think I saw it as we came down; I was on the look-out for it. If I'm right, it's only about a mile farther along. Confound those two Huns; in another five minutes we should have been well over the Lines.'

'Shall we be able to get through the wires, do you think?' asked Biggles.

'We shall not. I hear they have tightened things up a good deal along here lately, owing to escaped prisoners working their way back along the coast. Somebody told me they've got little bells hung all along the wire, and you can't touch it without ringing them. In any case, we should need rubber gloves because the Huns are electrifying their wire. No, I'm afraid we shall have to go round it.'

'Round it!'

'Yes, by swimming round it. It's been done before and it's our only chance.'

Biggles groaned. 'Fancy having to get into that water again! I'd sooner face the biggest formation of Huns that ever took the air. I had no idea water could be so cold. I nearly joined the Navy once; I'm thundering glad I didn't!' he grumbled.

'Don't grouse—we're lucky to be alive!' muttered Mark. 'Come on, now, no noise!'

Crouching and crawling, they began to wind their way through the dunes, taking a peep over the top whenever an opportunity presented itself in order to keep direction, which lay parallel to the shore. Sometimes they were able to walk a few yards, but on other occasions they had to worm their way like snakes across open spaces. Once they had to lie flat as a squad of troops, evidently a working party, passed within a few yards of them.

At last Mark raised himself up and peered forward. 'I think I can see the wire just ahead,' he breathed, 'but we can't get any farther along here. There must be a trench just in front, because I can hear people talking. We'd better get down to the water.'

'Lead on,' breathed Biggles. 'I can't be any colder than I am already!'

Dragging themselves along on their stomachs, often stopping to listen, they wormed their way to the water's edge.

'How far can you swim?' whispered Mark.

'I don't know,' admitted Biggles. 'I've never found it necessary to find out.'

'You'll have to chance it, then. I can swim pretty well any distance, but not when it's as cold as this. I was brought up by the sea. If you feel your strength giving out, hang on to my collar and we'll get around—or sink together. We shall have to get out just beyond the breakers, and then swim parallel to the coast. As soon as we see our own wire we'll come ashore. If we don't see it, we'll swim as far as we can. But the Lines can't be very far apart—come on!'

They plunged into the icy water and struck out through the blinding spray. Biggles paid little or no attention to the direction, but simply fixed his eyes on the black head bobbing in front of him and followed it.

How long they swam he did not know, but it seemed to be an eternity and he was just about to call out that he could go no farther when Mark turned shorewards. Biggles made one last despairing dash through the surf, and then lay panting and gasping like a stranded fish.

Mark seized him by the collar and dragged him out of the reach of the waves. 'Get up!' he snapped.

'Wait—a minute—let me—get—breath!' panted Biggles.

Mark dragged him roughly to his feet. 'Run!' he said. 'We shall have to start our blood moving, or we shall both be down with pneumonia. I think we're round both lots of wire; if we aren't, then we're unstuck, that's all about it.'

Without waiting for any more he set off at a steady trot along the sand, Biggles reeling behind him, their clothes squelching and discharging water at every step.

'*Halte-la*!'

They pulled up with a jerk as the challenge rang out.

'Friend—ami!' yelled Biggles desperately, but joyfully, for he knew the language was not German.

'*Attendez*!' called the voice, and they heard the jangle of military equipment. A dark figure, closely followed by several others, loomed up in the darkness in front of them, rifles and bayonets held at the ready.

'You do the talking!' growled Mark. 'I can't speak the lingo!'

'*Je suis—nous ont—Anglais*,' began Biggles in his best French. '*Aviateurs—aviateurs Anglais*.'

There was a sharp intake of breath, and a flashlight stabbed the darkness. The figures closed around them and they were hurried a short distance into a trench, and then into a dugout, where an officer in a blue uniform sat writing.

Quickly, in a strange mixture of English and broken French, Biggles told his story to the Belgian officer. He eyed them suspiciously at first, but at the end of the story he made a brief telephone call which seemed to satisfy him.

The dripping clothes were stripped off the two airmen,

53

blankets were produced, and boiling soup, in great basins, thrust into their hands.

An hour later a British staff officer stepped into the dug-out.

'Who are you?' he asked curtly, obviously suspicious. But suspicion quickly gave way to friendliness as the two airmen told their story.

Mark handed over his report, which, although wet, was still legible. 'I wish you'd get that back as quickly as you can, sir,' he said. 'We've been through some trouble to get it!'

'You can bring it yourself,' the officer told him. 'I have a car waiting a little way back. But you'll have to borrow some clothes if our Belgian friends can provide them. You can't put those wet ones on again!'

Dinner was in progress when Biggles and Mark, attired in mixed Belgian uniforms, arrived at their aerodrome They opened the mess door, and amid dead silence, with all eyes on them, they marched stiffly to the head of the table, where the C.O. sat, and apologized for being late for dinner.

The C.O. stared at them, while a babble of voices broke out, punctuated with laughs, that finally swelled into a roar in which everyone joined. Mark, who had seen such a scene before, knew that the laughter was simply the British way of expressing relief after they had been given up for lost.

But Biggles turned a pained face to the room.

'What's the joke?' he cried hotly. 'Do you think we're all dressed up for the fun of it?'

A fresh burst of laughter greeted his words.

'Everyone's glad to see you back, that's all!' said the C.O. 'And that's the chief thing. Did you get a report on the junction?'

'Yes, sir,' replied Mark.

'That's splendid! Sit down and have your dinners. You can tell us all about it afterwards!'

'I'M NOT GOING to pretend that I know much about it, but it seems to me that if the Huns are going to mass their squadrons—as apparently they are—we shall have to do the same or else be wiped out.' Biggles, having ventured an opinion for the first time since he joined the squadron, glanced up, half-expecting a remark about his inexperience.

'He's right!' exclaimed Mabs emphatically. 'I've been saying the same thing for the last month. Richthofen, they say, has grouped three squadrons together, including all the best pilots in the German Air Force. And, whether he has or not, we know for a fact that he's sailing up and down the Lines with thirty triplanes tagged on behind him. Who's going to face that bunch? Who's going to take on that little lot, I'd like to know? What chance has an ordinary Line patrol of three planes got if it bumps into that pack?'

'Rot!' snapped Captain Rayner, of C Flight. 'The more the merrier! Dive straight into the middle of them and the formation will go to pieces. It will take them all their time to avoid collision.'

'Don't kid yourself!' declared Captain Allen of B Flight. 'They've got this game weighed up nicely. They didn't wait for us to bump into them this morning—they bumped into us and we jolly soon knew about it!'

There was silence for a moment, due to the fact that B Flight had lost two machines that very morning through the menace they were discussing.

'I think it's a logical conclusion that if we start sending big patrols of twenty or thirty machines against them they'll start flying in fifties or more. Whatever we do, they will maintain numerical superiority, and at the finish formations will be flying in hundreds. A nice sort of game that will be!' declared Marriot disgustedly.

'Well, it may come to that some day, but if it does I hope I'm not here to see it,' observed Allen coldly. 'I——'

The ante-room door opened and an orderly appeared. 'Major Paynter's compliments, and will all officers please report to the squadron office at once?'

There was a general move towards the door.

The Major was in earnest conversation with Toddy, the Recording Officer, when they arrived, but he broke off and turned to face them as they entered.

'Well, gentlemen,' he said, 'I've some news for you, though whether you'll regard it as good or bad I don't know. Will all those officers who have had any experience of night-flying please take a pace to the front?'

Mabs, a pilot of B Flight and a pilot and observer of C Flight stepped forward.

'That's worse than I expected,' said the Major. 'Never mind; this is the position. Whether we like it or not, Wing have decided to carry out certain operations that can best be done at night. As you know, enemy scout squadrons have been concentrated opposite this sector of the Front, and our machines have neither the performance nor numerical strength of theirs. In these circumstances we are going to try to cripple them on the ground. It is thought that night raids will advisedly affect their morale, to say nothing of the damage we may cause on their machines or aerodromes. It's proposed to carry out the first raid on a very big scale; other squadrons will participate and keep the ball rolling all night. In order to put as large a number of machines in the air as possible, this squadron will take part in the raid, which will be on Douai Aerodrome, the headquarters of the Richthofen group.

'Fortunately, our machines are well adapted for night-flying, so for the next two nights I shall want all officers to put in as much practice in the air as possible. It's up to everyone to make himself proficient in the new conditions. Flares will be put out, and lectures will be arranged, which must be attended by all officers on the station. Has anyone any questions to ask?'

'I take it that the attack will be in the form of a bomb raid, sir?' said Biggles.

'We shall attack with all arms—heavy bombs, Cooper bombs, baby incendiaries, and machine-guns. Naturally, it is in our own interest to make a good job of the show; if things go according to plan, we shall meet with less opposition when we resume daylight patrols. That's all.'

'Well, that's the answer to the question!' observed Mark brightly, when they were outside.

'What question?'

'The thing we were talking about in the mess when the C.O. sent for us—the big Boche formations. We're going to swipe them on the ground!'

'Well, it may be all right,' replied Biggles thoughtfully, 'but we could have wiped them out in daylight shows if it comes to that. I'm thinking that there is one thing the staff people may have overlooked.'

'What's that?'

'You don't imagine for one moment that the Huns will take this night-strafing business lying down, do you? If I know anything about 'em they'll soon be showing us that it's a game two can play. You mark my words, they'll be over here the next night, handing us doses of our own medicine—in spoonfuls. I hope I'm mistaken, but I reckon things will be getting warmish here presently!'

'Well, the staff won't mind that; they won't be here,' observed Mark bitterly. 'I must say I don't fancy being archied at night; the flashes look ghastly. I've been told that they are a nice bright orange when they are close to you, and a beautiful dull crimson when they're some distance away.'

'We shall soon be able to see for ourselves whether your information is correct,' returned Biggles. 'As long as they're not pink with blue spots on 'em I don't mind!'

The weather on the night decided for the first raid was all that could be desired, considering the time of the year. There was no wind, and a new moon shone brightly in a clear, frosty, star-spangled sky, against which the hangars loomed as black silhouettes.

By the C.O.'s orders not a light gleamed anywhere, for every step was being taken to prevent information of the impending raid from reaching the enemy through the many spies whose duty it was to report such operations.

An engine roared suddenly in the darkness, and the end machine of a long line that stood in front of the hangars began to waddle, in the ungainly fashion of aeroplanes on the ground, towards the point allocated for the take-off; a dark red, intermittent flame, curled back from the exhaust-pipe.

'There goes Mabs,' said Biggles, who, with Mark his gunner, was standing by their machine.

The planes were to leave at five-minute intervals, which gave each aircraft a chance to get clear before the next one took off, and so lessened the chances of a collision either on the ground or in the air.

'Marriot goes next, and then McAngus, so we've got a quarter of an hour to wait,' went on Biggles. 'It's going to be perishing cold if I know anything about it,' he remarked, glancing up at the frosty sky. 'But there, we can't have it all ways. We shall at least be able to see where we are, and that's a lot better than groping our way in and out of clouds; that's bad enough in the day-time! Hallo There goes Marriot!'

A second machine taxied out and roared up into the darkness.

'Mabs has got to the Line—look!' said Mark, pointing to a cluster of twinkling yellow lights in the distant sky. 'That's archie!'

Lines of pale green balls seemed to be floating lazily upwards.

'Look at the onions,' he added, referring to the well-known enemy anti-aircraft device commonly known as flaming onions.

A third machine taxied out and vanished into the gloom.

'Well, there goes McAngus; we'd better see about getting started up,' said Biggles tersely.

They climbed into their cockpits, and mechanics ran to their wings and propeller.

'Switch off!'

'Off!'

The engine hissed and gurgled as the big propeller was dragged round to suck the gas into the cylinders.

'Contact!' cried the mechanic.

'Contact!' echoed Biggles.

There was a sharp explosion as the engine came to life; then it settled down to the musical purr peculiar to the Beardmore type.

For a few minutes they sat thus, giving the engine time to warm up; then Biggles opened the throttle a trifle and pointed to his right wing—the signal to the mechanics that he wanted it held in order to slew the machine round to the right. While a machine is on the ground with the engine running all orders are given by signals, for the human voice would be lost in the noise of the engine; even if it was heard, the words might not be distinguished clearly, and an accident result.

With his nose pointing towards the open aerodrome, Biggles waved both hands above his head, the signal to the mechanics to stand clear. The F.E. raced across the aerodrome, and then roared up into the starry night.

He did not waste time climbing for height over the aerodrome, but headed straight for the Lines, climbing as he went. Peering below, he could see the countryside about them almost as plainly as in day-time; here and there the lighted windows of cottages and farms stood out brightly in the darkness; far ahead he could see the track of the three preceding machines by the darting flashes of archie that followed them.

A British searchlight flashed a challenge to him as he passed over it, but Mark was ready, and replied at once with the colour of the night—a Very light that first burnt red and then changed to green. 'O.K.—O.K.,' flashed the searchlight in the Morse code, and they pursued their way for a time unmolested.

Biggles crouched a little lower in his seat as the first archies began to flash around them. It reached a crescendo as they crossed the Line, augmented by the inevitable flaming onions that rose up vertically from below like white-hot cannon-balls; but the turmoil soon faded away behind them as they sped on through the night over enemy territory, the Beardmore engine roaring sullen defiance. From time to time he peered below to pick up his landmarks, but for the most part he stared straight ahead, eyes probing the gloom for other machines.

The planes, of course, carried no lights, and although the chances of collision were remote, with machines of both sides going to and fro all the time, it was an ever-present possibility. In night raids it was usual for the machines taking part to return by a different route, or at a higher altitude to the one taken on the outward journey, and while machines adhered to this arrangement, collision was impossible.

Biggles was, of course, aware of this, but he kept an anxious eye on his line of flight in case an enemy machine had decided to take the same route as himself, but in the opposite direction, or in case Marriot or McAngus had got off their course.

Mark suddenly rose to his feet and pointed with outstretched finger. Far away, almost on the horizon, it seemed, a shaft of flame had leapt high into the air; the sky glowed redly from the conflagration, and Biggles knew that one of the machines preceding him had either reached its destination and set fire to the hangars, or had itself been shot down in flames.

The fire, however, served one good purposes, for it acted as a beacon that would guide them direct to their objective. It continued to blaze fiercely as they approached it, and presently the crew of the F.E. were able to see that it was actually on Douai Aerodrome. It looked like one of the hangars. Keeping on a line that would bring him right over it Biggles throttled back and began gliding down.

Orders had stated that machines should descend as low as five hundred feet, if necessary, to be reasonably sure of hitting the target; but the thrill of the game was in his blood, and he no longer thought of orders. At five hundred feet he shoved the throttle open wide, and, pushing the stick forward, swept down so low that Mark, in the front seat, stared back over his shoulder in amazement.

The instant he opened his throttle an inferno seemed to break loose about the machine. Anti-aircraft guns and even field-guns situated on the edge of the aerodrome spat their hate; machine-guns rattled like castanets, the tracer bullets cutting white pencil lines through the darkness. Out of the corner of his eyes Biggles saw Mark crouch low over his gun and heard it break into its staccato chatter.

He grabbed the bomb-toggle as the first hangar leapt into view, and, steadying the machine until the ridge of the roof appeared at the junction of his fuselage and the leading edge of the lower plane, he jerked it upwards—one, two.

Two 112-pound bombs swung off their racks, and the machine wobbled as it was relieved of their weight. Straight along over the hangars the F.E. roared, while Mark stood up and threw the baby incendiaries overboard.

When they came to the end of the line, Biggles zoomed up in a wide turn and tore out of the vicinity, twisting and turning like a wounded bird. Only when the furious bombardment had died away behind them did he lean over the side of the cockpit and look back at the aerodrome. His heart leapt with satisfaction, for two hangars were blazing furiously, the flames leaping high into the sky and casting a lurid glow on the surrounding landscape.

A body of men was working feverishly to get some aeroplanes out of one of the burning hangars; a machine that had evidently been standing outside when the attack was launched had been blown over on its back; several figures were prone on the ground, and one man was crawling painfully away from the heat of the fire.

'Well, that should make things easy for the others; they can't very well miss that little bonfire!' mused Biggles with satisfaction. Shells started bursting again in the air on the far side of the aerodrome, and he knew that Captain Allen, in the leading machine of B Flight, was approaching to carry on the good work.

'If our people are going to keep that up all night, those

fellows down there will have nasty tastes in their mouths by the morning!' called Biggles, smiling; but the next instant the smile had given way to a frown of anxiety as a new note crept into the steady drone of the engine.

Looking back over his shoulder his heart missed a beat as he saw a streamer of flame sweeping aft from one of the cylinders. Mark had seen it, too, and was staring at him questioningly, his face shining oddly pink in the glow.

Biggles throttled back a trifle and the flame became smaller, but the noise continued and the machine began to vibrate.

'It feels as if they've either blown one of my jampots off or else a bullet has knocked a hole through the water jacket,' he yelled. 'If it will last for another half-hour, all right! If it doesn't, we're in the soup!'

With the throttle retarded he was creeping along at a little more than stalling speed, so he tried opening it again gently. Instantly a long streamer of fire leapt out of the engine, and the vibration became so bad that it threatened to tear the engine from its bearers. With a nasty sinking feeling in the pit of his stomach he snatched the throttle back to its original position, and shook his head at Mark as the only means he had of telling him that he was unable to overcome the trouble.

The noise increased until it became a rattling jar, as if a tin of nails was being shaken. A violent explosion behind caused him to catch his breath, and he retarded the throttle still farther, with a corresponding loss of speed. He had to tilt his nose down in order to prevent the machine from stalling, and he knew that he was losing height too fast to reach home.

He moistened his lips and stared into the darkness ahead, for it had been arranged that a 'lighthouse' should flash a beam at regular intervals to guide the bombers back to their nest. Watching, he saw a glow on the skyline wax and wane, but it was still far away.

He looked at his altimeter; it registered two thousand five hundred feet. Could he do it? He thought not, but he could try.

The rattle behind him and the vibration grew rapidly

62

wo se; it became a definite pulsating jolt that threatened to shake the machine to pieces at any moment. But he could see the Lines in the distance now, or rather, the trench system, where the patrols on either side were watching or trying to repair their barbed wire.

Two loud explosions in quick succession and a blinding sheet of flame leapt from the engine and made him throttle right back with frantic haste.

'Well, if we're down, we're down!' he muttered savagely. 'But I'm not going to sit up here and be fried to death for anybody; the Huns can shoot us if they like when we're on the ground, and that's better than being roasted like a joint of meat on the spit.'

Looking behind him he could see flames from the engine playing on his tail unit, and he knew that if he tried to remain in the air it was only a matter of seconds before the whole thing took fire. He switched off altogether and began gliding down through the darkness, straining his eyes in an effort to see what lay beneath.

In the uncanny silence he could hear the reports of the guns on the ground, and even hear the rattle of machine-gun fire. A searchlight probed the sky like a trembling white finger, searching for him, and archie began to illuminate the surrounding blackness.

Mark, the ever-practical, was calmly preparing for the inevitable end, and even in that desperate moment Biggles wondered if there was anything that could shake Mark out of his habitual calmness. He picked up the machine-guns, one after the other, and threw them overboard; the Huns would be welcome to what was left of them after their eight-hundred-foot fall. The ammunition drums followed. He tore up his maps, threw them into the air and watched them swirl away aft.

Biggles felt in the canvas pocket inside the cockpit, then took out his own maps, ripped them across, and sent the pieces after Mark's. He thrust his loaded Very pistol into his pocket in readiness to send a shot into the petrol tank of the machine as soon as they were on the ground—providing they were not knocked out in the crash.

The destruction of his machine to prevent it falling into

63

the hands of the enemy is the first duty of an airman who lands in hostile territory.

The sky around them became an inferno of darting flames and hurtling metal. Several pieces of shrapnel struck the machine, and it quivered like a terrified horse. Once the F.E. was nearly turned upside down by a terrific explosion under the port wing-tip. 400—300—200 feet ran the altimeter. Mark was leaning over the side staring into the blackness below them.

Biggles could distinguish nothing; the earth looked like a dark indigo stain, broken only by the flashes of guns and the intermittent spurts of machine-guns. He no longer looked at his altimeter, for he knew he was too low for it to be of any assistance; he could only keep his eyes glued below and hope for the best.

Suddenly, the shadow that was the earth swept up to meet him. He pulled the joy-stick back until the machine was flying on even keel. It began to sink as it lost flying speed, then staggered like a drunken animal. He lifted his knees to his chin, covered his face with his arms, and waited for the end. For a moment there was silence, broken only by the faint hum of the wires and the rumble of the guns.

Crash! With a crunching, tearing, rending scream of protest, the machine struck the ground and subsided in a heap of debris. The nacelle, in which the crew sat, buried its nose into the earth, reared up, then turned turtle.

Biggles soared through space and landed with a dull squelch in a sea of mud, but he had scrambled to his feet in an instant, wiping the slime from his eyes with the backs of his gauntlets.

'Mark—Mark!' he hissed. 'Where are you, Mark? Are you hurt, old man?'

'Hold hard, I'm coming! Don't make such a row, you fool!' snarled Mark, dragging himself clear of the debris and unwinding a wire that had coiled around his neck.

Rat-tat-tat-tat. Rat-tat-tat-tat.

A Very light soared upwards, and half a dozen machine-guns began their vicious stutter somewhere near at hand; bullets began splintering into the mangled wreck of the machine and zipping into the mud like a swarm of angry hornets.

'Come on, let's get out of this!' gasped Mark. 'Run for it; the artillery will open up any second!'

'Run! Where to?' panted Biggles.

'Anywhere—to get away from here!' snapped Mark, slithering and sliding through the ooze.

Whee-e-e—Bang! The first shell arrived with the noise of an express train and exploded with a roar like the end of the world. Biggles took a flying leap into a shell-hole and wormed his way into the mud at the bottom like a mole. He grunted as Mark landed on top of him.

'Why—the dickens—don't you look—where you're going!' he spluttered, as they squelched side by side in the sludge while the shell-torn earth rocked under the onslaught from the artillery.

'We're all right here,' announced Mark firmly. 'They say a shell never lands in the same place twice.'

'I wish I knew that for a fact,' muttered Biggles. 'This is what comes of night-flying. Night birds, eh? Great jumping mackerel, we're a couple of owls all right; an owl's got enough sense to stay——'

'Shut up!' snarled Mark, as the bombardment grew less intense, and suddenly died away. 'Let's see where we are.' he whispered, as an eerie silence settled over the scene.

'See where we are? Have you any idea where we are?'

'Hark!'

They held their breaths and listened, but no sound reached their ears.

'I thought I heard someone coming,' breathed Mark. 'This is awful, not knowing which side of the lines we're on!'

They crept up to the lip of the shell-crater and stared into the surrounding darkness. A Very light soared upwards from a spot about a hundred yards away. Biggles, peering under his hand in the glare, distinctly saw a belt of barbed wire a few yards away on their left. Mark, who was looking in the other direction, gripped his arm in a vice-like clutch.

'Huns!' he whispered. 'There's a party of them coming this way. I could tell them by the shape of their helmets. Come on, this way!'

They started crawling warily towards the wire, but when they reached it, finding no opening, they commenced crawling parallel with it, freezing into a death-like stillness whenever a Very light cast its weird glow over the scene.

'Those Huns were coming from the opposite direction, so this should be our side,' muttered Mark.

'Don't talk,' whispered Biggles, 'let's keep going—this looks like a gap in the wire.'

By lying flat on the ground so that the obstruction was silhouetted against the sky, they could see a break in the ten feet wide belt of barbed wire, where it had evidently been torn up by shell-fire. They crawled through the breach, then paused to listen with straining ears.

'I can hear someone talking ahead of us; they must be in a trench,' whispered Mark.

'So can I; let's get closer,' whispered Biggles. 'Ssh— there it is! I can see the parapet. We shall have to go carefully, or we may be shot by our own fellows.' He raised himself on his hands and was about to call out—in fact, he had opened his mouth to do so—when a sound reached their ears that seemed to freeze the blood in their veins.

It was a harsh, coarse voice, speaking in a language they did not understand, but which they had no difficulty in recognizing as German. It came from the parapet a few yards in front of them.

A line of bayonets and then a body of men rose up in the darkness at the edge of the trench; there was no mistaking the coal-scuttle helmets.

Neither of the airmen spoke; as one man they sank to the ground, forcing themselves into the cold mud, and lay motionless. Heavy footsteps squelched through the mud towards them; a voice was speaking in a low undertone. Nearer and nearer they came, until Biggles felt the muscles of his back retract to receive the stabbing pain of a bayonet-thrust. He nearly cried out as a heavy foot descended on his hand, but his gauntlet and the soft mud under it saved the bones from being broken. The German

66

stumbled, recovered, half-glanced over his shoulder to see what had tripped him; but, seeing what he supposed to be a corpse, turned and walked quickly after the others.

'Phew!' gasped Biggles, as the footsteps receded into the distance.

'Let's get out of this!' muttered Mark. 'They may be back any moment. Another minute and we should have walked straight into their trench. Hark!'

The hum of an F.E. reached their ears, and although they could not see it they could follow its path of flight by the archie bursts and the sound. It was coming from the direction of the German trench. It passed straight over them; the archie died away, and presently the sound faded into the night.

'That's one of our fellows going home, so it gives us our direction if we can only find a way through our own wire. If there isn't a gap, we're sunk; so we might crawl along this blinking wire to Switzerland!'

'Ssh!'

Once more the sound of footsteps reached them from somewhere near at hand, but they could see nothing.

'I can't stand much more of this!' growled Biggles. 'It's giving me the creeps. I've just crawled over somebody—or something that was somebody.'

Bang! They both jumped and then lay flat as another Very light curved high into the air; in its dazzling light Biggles distinctly saw a group of German soldiers, evidently a patrol, standing quite still, not more than fifty yards away. Suddenly he remembered something. He groped in his pocket, whipped out his own Very pistol, took careful aim, and fired. The light in the air went out at the same moment. The shot from Biggles' pistol dropped in the mud a hundred yards away, where it lay hissing in a cloud of red smoke that changed gradually to a ghastly, livid green.

'You fool, what are you at?' snarled Mark. 'I thought I was shot.'

'Didn't you see those Huns? I bet I've made them jump!'

'They'll probably make us jump in a minute!' retorted Mark.

'Would have done if I hadn't fired that Very light at 'em, you mean!' retorted Biggles. 'Nothing like getting in the first shot. Makes the other fellow scary. We've been walked over by one crowd and treated as bloomin' doormats. I don't want a second dose of that!'

'You'll get a dose of something else if those Huns poodle along here to inquire what the fireworks are for!' replied Mark.

'If!' jeered Biggles. 'I'll bet those chaps are legging it for home for all they're worth. An' I don't blame 'em. I'd do the same myself if I jolly well knew where home was.'

'You'll never live to see home again if you don't stop playing the silly ass!' growled Mark. 'And now shut up and listen. See if you can hear anybody talking in a language we understand.'

For some time the two airmen remained still, lying on the ground and listening intently for the sound of voices. But they could hear nothing save the occasional banging of rifles. At last Biggles grew impatient.

'Well, I'm not going to stay messing about here any longer!' he snapped. 'We'll settle things one way or the other. It will start to get light presently, and then we're done for. I believe that's our wire just in front of us. What about letting out a shout to see if our fellows are within earshot?'

'The Huns will hear us, too.'

'I can't help that. Hold tight, I'm going to yell. Hallo, there!' he bellowed. 'Is anybody about?'

A reply came from a spot so close that Biggles instinctively ducked.

'What are you bleating abart?' said a Cockney voice calmly. 'You come any closer to me and I'll give you something to holler for. You can't catch me on that hop!'

Bang! A rifle blazed in the darkness, not ten yards away, and a bullet whistled past Biggles' head.

'Hi! That's enough of that!' he shouted. 'We're British officers, I tell you—fliers. We crashed outside the wire and can't get through. Come and show us the way!'

'Why didn't you say so before?' came the reply. 'You might 'ave got 'urt. 'Old 'ard a minute! But you keep your 'ands up, and no half-larks!'

Silence fell.

'He's either coming himself, or he's gone to fetch someone,' muttered Mark. 'We can't blame him for being suspicious. He must have been in a listening-post, which is where people shoot first and ask questions afterwards. The Huns get up to all sorts of tricks.'

'Where are you, you fellows?' suddenly said a quiet voice near them.

'Here we are!' answered Biggles.

'Stand fast—I'm coming.'

An officer, revolver in hand, closely followed by half a dozen Tommies wearing the unmistakable British tin helmets, loomed up suddenly in the darkness.

'How many of you are there?' said the voice.

'Two,' replied Biggles shortly.

'All right, follow me—and don't make a row about it.'

Squelching through the ooze, they followed the officer through a zigzag track in the wire. The Tommies closed in behind them. A trench, from which projected a line of bayonets, lay across their path, but at a word from their escort the rifles were lowered, and the two airmen half-slipped and half scrambled into the trench. The beam of a flash-lamp cut through the darkness and went slowly over their faces and uniforms.

'You look a couple of pretty scarecrows, I must say,' said a voice, with a chuckle. 'Come into my dugout and have a rest. I'll send a runner to headquarters with a request that they ring up your squadron and tell them you're safe. What have you been up to?'

'Oh—er—night-flying, that's all. Just night-flying!' said Biggles airily.

'BEG PARDON, SIR, but Major Paynter wishes to speak to you, sir.'

Biggles glanced up, folded the letter he was reading, and put it in his pocket. 'On the 'phone, do you mean?' he asked the mess waiter, who had delivered the message.

'No, sir, in his office, Mr. Todd rang up to say would you go along right away.'

'All right, Collins, thanks.' Biggles picked up his cap as he went through the hall and walked quickly along the well-worn path to the squadron office. Two people were present in addition to the C.O. when he entered—one a red-tabbed staff-officer, and the other, a round-faced, cheerful-looking civilian in a black coat and bowler hat. Biggles saluted.

'Just make sure the door is closed, will you, Bigglesworth?' began the C.O. 'Thanks. This is Major Raymond, of Wing Headquarters.'

'How do you do, sir?' said Biggles to the staff officer, wondering why the C.O. did not introduce the civilian, and what he was doing there.

'I want to have a few words with you, Bigglesworth, on a very delicate subject,' went on the C.O. rather awkwardly. 'Er—I, or I should say the squadron, has been asked to undertake an—er—operation of the greatest importance. It is a job that will have to be done single-handed, and I am putting the proposition to you first because you have shown real enthusiasm in your work since you've been with us, and because you have extricated yourself from one or two difficult situations entirely by your own initiative. The job in hand demands both initiative and resource.'

'Thank you, sir.'

'Not a bit. Now, this is the proposition. The operation briefly, consists in taking an—er—gentleman over the Lines, landing him at a suitable spot, and then returning home. It is probable that you will have to go over the Lines again afterwards, either the same night or at a subsequent date, and pick him up from the place where you landed him.'

'That does not seem diffi——'

Major Paynter held up his hand.

'Wait!' he said. 'Let me finish. It is only fair that I should warn you that in the event of your being forced down on the wrong side of the Lines, or being captured in any way, you would probably be shot. Even if you had to force-land in German territory on the return journey, with no one in the machine but yourself, it is more than likely that the enemy would suspect your purpose and subject you to rigorous interrogation. And if the enemy could wring the truth from you—that you had been carrying a Secret Service agent—they would be justified in marching you before a firing squad.'

'I understand. Very good, sir. I'll go.'

'Thank you, Bigglesworth! The gentleman here with Major Raymond will be your passenger. It would be well for you to meet him now, as you will not see him again in daylight, and you should be able to identify each other.'

Biggles walked over to the civilian and held out his hand. 'Pleased to meet you!' he said.

The spy—for Biggles had no delusions about the real nature of the work on hand—smiled and wrung his hand warmly. He was a rather fat, jovial-looking little man with a huge black moustache; in no way was he like the character Biggles would have expected for such work.

'Well, I think that's all for the present, Raymond,' went on the C.O. 'Let me know the details as soon as you can. I'll have another word with you, Bigglesworth, before you go.'

Biggles saluted as the staff officer departed with his

civilian companion, and then turned his attention again to Major Paynter, who was staring thoughtfully out of the window.

'I want you to see this thing in its true perspective,' resumed the C.O. 'We are apt to think spying is rather dirty work. It may be, from the strictly military point of view, but one should not forget that it needs as much nerve —if not more—than anything a soldier is called upon to face. A soldier may be killed, wounded, or made prisoner. But a spy's career can only have one ending if he's caught —the firing squad! He does not die a man's death in the heat of battle; he is shot like a dog against a brick wall. That's the result of failure. If he succeeds, he gets no medals, honour or glory. Silence surrounds him always.

'And most of these men work for nothing. Take that man you've just seen, for instance. He is, of course, a Frenchman. In private life he's a schoolmaster at Aille, which is now in territory occupied by the enemy. He worked his way across the frontier into Holland, and then to France, via England, to offer his services to his country. He asks no reward. There's courage and self-sacrifice, if you like. Remember that when he's in your machine. His knowledge of the country around Aille makes his services particularly valuable. If he gets back safely this time—he has already made at least one trip—he will go again. And so it will go on, until one day he will not come back.

'As far as you're concerned as his pilot, you need have no scruples. Most of the leading French pilots have taken their turns for special missions, as these affairs are called. For obvious reasons, only the best pilots, those of proven courage, are chosen for the work. Well, I think that's all. I'll let you know the details, the date and time, later on. Don't mention this matter to anybody, except, of course, your flight-commander, who will have to know.'

Biggles bumped into Mapleton, his flight-commander, just outside the office.

'What's on?' asked Mabs quietly. 'Special Mission?'

Biggles nodded.

'I thought so. For the love of Mike be careful! You've only got to make one bloomer at that game, and all the king's horses and all the king's men couldn't save you. I did one once, and that was enough for me. No more, thank you!'

'Why, did things go wrong?' inquired Biggles, as they walked towards the mess.

'Wrong! It was worse than that. In the first place, the cove refused to get out of the machine when we got there; his nerves petered out. He couldn't speak English, and I can't speak French, so I couldn't tell him what I thought of him. When I tried to throw him out he kicked up such a row that it brought all the Huns for miles to the spot. I had to get off in a hurry, I can tell you, bringing the blighter back with me. But some of these fellows have been over no end of times, and they have brought back, or sent back, information of the greatest importance. They have to carry a basket of pigeons with them, and they release one every time they get information worth while. How would you like to walk about amongst the Boche with a pigeon up your coat? It's only got to give one coo and you're sunk. The French pilots have had a go at it. Vedrines, the pre-war pilot, did several shows. When the War broke out the French expected great things of him, and when he just faded into insignificance they began saying nasty things about him. But he was doing special missions, and those are things people don't talk about.'

'Well, if my bowler-hatted bird starts any trouble I'll give him a thick ear!' observed Biggles.

'Oh, he'll be all right, I should think!' replied Mabs. 'The landing is the tricky part. The Huns know all about this spy-dropping game, and they do their best to catch people in the act by laying traps in likely landing-fields, such as by digging trenches across the field and then covering them up with grass so that you can't see them. When you land—zonk! Another scheme is to stretch wire across the field, which has a similar result.'

'Sounds cheerful! And there are no means of knowing whether a trap has been laid in the field that you have to land on?'

'Not until you land,' grinned Mabs.

'That's a fat lot of good!' growled Biggles. 'Well, we shall see. Many thanks for the tips!'

'That's all right. My only advice is, don't let them catch you alive, laddie. Remember, they shoot you as well as the fellow you are carrying if you're caught. They treat you both alike!'.

'They'll have to shoot me to catch me!' replied Biggles grimly.

The hands of the mess clock pointed to the hour of nine when, a few evenings later, Biggles finished his after-dinner coffee, and, collecting his flying kit from its peg in the hall, strolled towards the door.

Mark Way, who had followed him out of the room, noted these proceedings with surprise. 'What's the idea?' he asked, reaching for his own flying kit.

'I've a little job to do—on my own. I can't talk about it. Sorry, old lad!' replied Biggles, and departed. He found Major Raymond and his civilian acquaintance waiting on the tarmac. In accordance with his instructions to the flight-sergeant, his F.E.2b had been wheeled out and the engine was ticking over quietly.

'Remember, he's doing the job for us, not for the French,' Major Raymond told him quietly. 'He's going to dynamite a bridge over the Aisne near the point that I told you about yesterday,' he went on, referring to a conversation on the previous day at which the details had been arranged. 'He's asked me to tell you not to worry about his return. He's quite willing for you to leave him to work his own way back across the frontier, although naturally he'd be glad if you would pick him up again later on.'

'How long will he be doing his job, sir?' asked Biggles.

'It's impossible to say. So much depends on the conditions when he gets there—whether or not there are guards at the bridge, and so on. If it is all clear, he might do the job in half an hour, or an hour. On the other hand, he may be two or three days, waiting for his opportunity. Why do you ask?'

'I was thinking that if he wasn't going to be very long, I might wait for him?'

The major shook his head. 'It isn't usually done that way,' he said. 'It's too risky!'

'The risk doesn't seem to be any greater than making another landing.'

'Wait a minute and I'll ask him,' said the major.

He had a quick low conversation with the secret agent, and then returned to Biggles.

'He says the noise of your engine would attract attention if you waited, and it would not be advisable for you to switch off,' he reported. 'All the same, he asked me to tell you that he'd be very grateful if you would pick him up a few hours afterwards—it would save him three weeks' or a month's anxious work getting through Holland. He suggests that you allow him as much time as possible, in case he's delayed. If you'll return at the first glimmer of dawn he'll try to be back by then. If he's not there, go home and forget about him. He suggests dawn because it may save you actually landing. If you can't see him in the field, or on the edge of the field, don't land. If he is there, he'll show himself. That seems to be a very sensible arrangement, and a fair one for both parties.'

'More than fair,' agreed Biggles. 'If he's got enough nerve to dodge about amongst the Huns with a stick of dynamite in one pocket and a pigeon in the other, I ought to have enough nerve to fetch him back!'

'Quite! Still, he's willing to leave it to you.'

Biggles strolled across and shook hands with the man, who did not seem in the least concerned about the frightful task he was about to undertake. He was munching a biscuit contentedly.

'It is an honour to know you,' Biggles said. And he meant it.

'It is for *La France*,' answered the man simply.

'Well, I'm ready when you are!'

'*Bon*. Let us go,' was the reply. And they climbed into their seats.

Biggles noted with amazement that his passenger did not even wear flying kit. He wore the same dark suit as before, and the bowler hat, which he jammed hard on. He carried two bundles, and Biggles did not question what they contained; he thought he knew. Pigeons and dynamite were a curious mixture, he thought, as he settled himself into his seat.

He could hardly repress a smile as his eye fell on the unusual silhouette in the front cockpit. There was something queer about going to war in a bowler hat. Then something suspiciously like a lump came into his throat at the thought of the simple Frenchman, unsoldierly though he was in appearance, risking his all to perform an act of service to his country. He made up his mind that if human hands could accomplish it, he would bring his man safely back.

'I am ready, my little cabbage. Pour the sauce!' cried the man. And Biggles laughed aloud at the command to open the throttle. There was something very likeable about this fellow who could start on a mission of such desperate peril so casually.

'Won't you be frozen?' asked Biggles.

'It is not of the importance,' replied the Frenchman. 'We shall not be of the long time.'

'As you like,' shouted Biggles, and waved the wing-tip mechanics away. The engines roared as he opened the throttle, and a moment later he was in the air heading towards the Lines. In spite of the cold the little man still stood in his seat, with his coat-collar turned up, gazing below at the dark shadow of his beloved France.

Presently the archie began to tear the air about them. It was particularly vicious, and Biggles crouched a little lower in his seat. The spy leaned back towards him and cupped his hands around his mouth. 'How badly they shoot, these Boche!' he called cheerfully.

Biggles regarded him stonily. The fellow obviously had no imagination, for the bombardment was bad enough to make a veteran quail.

'He can't understand, that's all about it! Great jumping cats, I'd hate to be with him in what he would call good shooting!' he thought, and then turned his attention to the task of finding his way to the landing-ground they had decided upon. For his greatest fear was that he would be unable to locate it in the darkness, although he had marked it down as closely as he could by means of surrounding landmarks.

He picked out a main road, lying like a grey ribbon across the landscape, followed it until it forked, took the left fork, and then followed that until it disappeared into a wood. On the far side of the wood he made out the unmistakable straight track of a railway line, running at right angles to it. He followed this in turn, until the lights of a small town appeared ahead. Two roads converged upon it, and somewhere between the two roads and the railway line lay the field in which he had been instructed to land.

He intended to follow his instructions to the letter, knowing that the authorities must have a good reason for their choice. Possibly they knew from secret agents who were working, or had worked, in the vicinity, that the field had not been wired, or that it had not even fallen under the suspicion of the enemy. He dismissed the matter from his mind and concentrated upon the task of finding the field and landing the machine in it.

He cut the engine and commenced a long glide down. He glided as slowly as he could without losing flying speed so that possible watchers on the ground would not hear the wind vibrating in his wires, which they might if he came down too quickly. The spy was leaning over the side of the cockpit, watching the proceedings with interest. Then, as Biggles suddenly spotted the field and circled carefully towards it, the Frenchman picked up his parcels and placed them on the seat with no more concern than a passenger in an omnibus or railway train prepares to alight.

Biggles could see the field clearly now—a long, though not very wide strip of turf. He side-slipped gently to bring the F.E. dead in line with the centre of the field, glided like a wraith over the tops of the trees that bounded the northern end, and then flattened out.

The machine sank slowly, the wheels trundled over the rough turf—with rather a lot of noise, Biggles thought— the tail-skid dragged, and the machine ran to a stop after one of the best landings he had ever made in his life. He sank back limply, realizing that the tension of the last few minutes had been intense.

'Thank you, my little cabbage!' whispered the Frenchman, and glided away into the darkness.

For a moment or two Biggles could hardly believe that he had gone, so quietly and swiftly had he disappeared. For perhaps a minute he sat listening, but he could hear nothing, save the muffled swish of his idling propeller. He stood up and stared into the darkness on all sides, but there was no sign of life; not a light showed anywhere. As far as his late passenger was concerned, the ground might have opened and swallowed him up.

'Well, I might as well be going!' he decided.

There was no need for him to turn in order to take off. He had plenty of 'run' in front of him, and the engine roared as he opened the throttle and swept up into the night. He almost laughed with relief as the earth dropped away below him.

It had all been absurdly easy, and the reaction left him with a curious feeling of elation—a joyful sensation that the enemy had been outwitted. 'These things aren't so black as they're painted!' was his unspoken thought as he headed back towards the Lines. He crossed them in the usual flurry of archie, and ten minutes later taxied up to his flight hangar and switched off. He glanced at his watch. Exactly fifty minutes had elapsed since he and his companion had taken off from the very spot on which the machine now stood, and it seemed incredible that in that interval of time he had actually landed in German territory and unloaded a man who, for all he knew, might now be dead or in a prison cell awaiting execution. He hoped fervently that the second half of his task might prove as simple. He climbed stiffly to the ground and met Mabs and Mark, who had evidently heard him land.

'How did you get on?' asked Mabs quickly.

'Fine! If I'd known you were waiting I'd have brought you a bunch of German primroses; there were some growing in the field.'

'You'd better turn in and get some sleep,' Mabs advised him.

78

'Yes, I might as well—for a bit.'

'For a bit? What do you mean?'

'I'm going over again presently to fetch my bowler-hatted pal back!'

Biggles condemned the spy, the authorities in general, and the Germans in particular, to purgatory when, at the depressing hour of five o'clock the following morning, his batman aroused him from a deep, refreshing sleep.

It was bitterly cold, and the stars were still twinkling brightly in a wintry sky; a thick layer of white frost covered everything and wove curious patterns on the window-panes. It was one of those early spring frosts that remind us that the winter is not yet finished.

'What an hour to be hauled out of bed!' he grumbled, half-regretting his rash promise to fetch his man. But a cup of hot coffee and some toast put a fresh complexion on things, and he hummed cheerfully as he strode briskly over the crisp turf towards the sheds. He had told the flight-sergeant to detail two mechanics to 'stand by,' and he found them shivering in their greatcoats, impatiently awaiting his arrival. 'All right, get her out,' he said sharply, and between them they dragged the F.E. out on to the tarmac. 'Start her up,' he went on, tying a thick woollen muffler round his neck and then pulling on his flying kit.

Five minutes later he was in the air again, heading towards the scene of action.

The sky began to grow pale in the east, and, following the same landmarks that he had used before, he had no difficulty in finding his way. The first flush of dawn was stealing across the sky as he approached the field, but the earth was still bathed in deep blue and purple shadows.

He throttled back and began gliding down, eyes probing the shadows, seeking for the field and the little man. He picked out the field, but the spy was nowhere in sight, and Biggles' heart sank with apprehension, for he had developed a strong liking for him. He continued to circle for a few minutes, losing height slowly, eyes running over the surrounding country. Suddenly they stopped and remained fixed on the one spot where a movement had attracted his attention. Something had flashed dully, but for a second he could not make out what it was.

A fresh turn brought him nearer, and then he saw distinctly—horses—mounted troops—Uhlans. A troop of them was standing quietly under a clump of leafless trees near the main road, not more than a couple of hundred yards away from the field. He saw others, and small groups of infantry, at various points around the field, concealing themselves as well as the sparse cover would permit.

His lips turned dry. No wonder the little man was not there. For some reason or other, possibly because the mission had been successful, the whole countryside was being watched. Yet, he reasoned, the very presence of the troops suggested that the little man had not been caught. If he had been taken there would be no need for the troops —unless they were waiting for the plane. Well, the little man was not there, so there was no point in landing. He might as well go home. He had no intention of stepping into the trap.

He was within two hundred feet of the ground, and actually had his hand on the throttle to open his engine again, when a figure burst from the edge of the field and waved its arms. Biggles drew in his breath with a sharp hiss, for the Uhlans had started to move forward. He flung the control-stick over to the left, and, holding up the plane's nose with right rudder, dropped like a stone in a vertical sideslip towards the field.

Never in his life had his nerves been screwed up to such a pitch. His heart hammered violently against his ribs but his brain was clear, and he remained cool and collected. He knew that only perfect judgment and timing could save the situation. The Uhlans were coming at a canter; already they were in the next field.

With his eyes on the man he skimmed over the tops of the trees, put the machine on even keel, and began to flatten out. Then a remarkable thing happened—an occurrence so unexpected and so inexplicable that for a moment he was within an ace of taking off again. A second figure had sprung out of the ditch behind the man in the field and started to run towards him. The new-comer wore a black coat and bowler hat. He did not run towards the machine, but raced towards the man who had been waving, and who was now making for the F.E.

Up to this moment it had not occurred to Biggles for one instant that the man who had been waving was not his little man, and when the second figure appeared his calculations were thrown into confusion. The man in the bowler hat was the spy, there was no doubt of that, for he was now close enough for his face and figure to be recognized. Who, then, was the other?

The Frenchman seemed to know, for as he closed on him he flung up his right hand. There was a spurt of flame. The other flung up his arms and pitched forward on to his face.

Biggles began to see daylight. The thing was an artfully prepared trap. The first man who had showed himself was a decoy, an imposter to lure him to his death. The real spy had been lying in the hedge bottom, not daring to show himself with so many troops about, hoping that he, Biggles, would not land, which would have been in accordance with their plans.

From his position the spy had seen the decoy break cover, and knew his purpose. So he had exposed himself to warn his flying partner, even at the expense of his own life.

The knowledge made Biggles still more determined to save him, although he could see it was going to be a matter of touch-and-go. The decoy lay where he had fallen, and the little Frenchman, still wearing his bowler, was sprinting as fast as his legs could carry him towards the now taxi- ing machine.

But the Uhlans were already putting their horses at the hedge, not a hundred yards away. Shots rang out, the sharp whip-like cracks of cavalry carbines splitting the still morning air. Bullets hummed like angry wasps, one tearing through the machine with a biting jar that made Biggles wince.

'Come on!' he roared, unable to restrain himself, and he opened the throttle slightly.

The little man's face was red with exertion, and he was puffing hard. He took a flying leap at the nose of the F.E. and dragged himself up on to the edge of the cockpit. '*Voila!* We have made it, my little mushroom!' he gasped, And then, as Biggles jammed the throttle wide open, he pitched head first inside.

The Uhlans were galloping towards them, crouching low on the backs of their mounts, and spurring them to greater efforts. There was no time to turn. Biggles did the only thing possible. He shoved the joy-stick forward and charged. He caught a glimpse of swerving horses and flashing carbines straight in front of him; then he pulled the stick back into his stomach, flinching from what seemed must end in collision.

He relaxed limply as the F.E. zoomed upwards, and shook his head as if unable to believe that they were actually in the air. For the last two or three minutes he had not been conscious of actual thought. He had acted purely on instinct, throwing the whole strain on his nerves.

A round, good-humoured face appeared above the edge of the forward cockpit. The spy caught his eye and grinned. '*Bon!*' he shouted. 'That's the stuff, my little cabbage!'

Major Raymond was watching on the tarmac when they landed. His face beamed with delight when he saw they were both in the machine.

'How did it go?' he asked the little Frenchman quickly.

'*Pouf!* Like that!' said the spy. 'The bridge is no more, and, thanks to my little specimen here, I can now have my coffee at home instead of with the pigsheads over the way.'

'Have a close call, Bigglesworth?' asked the major, becoming serious.

'We did, sir!' admitted Biggles. 'I think I shall fly in a bowler hat in future—they seem to be lucky!'

'Ah! But those Boches are cunning ones!' muttered the Frenchman. 'They hunt for me, but I am in the ditch like a rabbit. They know the aeroplane will come, so they find another man to make my little artichoke land. He lands—so. I think furiously. *La, la*, it is simple. I shoot, and then I run. My Jingoes, how I run! Pish. We win, and here we are. I think we will go again some day, eh?' He beamed at Biggles.

'Perhaps!' agreed Biggles, but without enthusiasm. 'I've had all I want for a little while, though!'

'Pish!' laughed the spy. 'It was nothing! Just a little excitement to—how you say?—warm the blood.'

'Warm the blood!' exclaimed Biggles. 'When I want to do that I'll do it in front of the mess-room fire, thanks! Your sort of warm gets me overheated!'

BIGGLES' FACE wore a curious expression as he gazed down upon the blue-green panorama four thousand feet below. The day was fine and clear, and recent rain had washed the earth until roads and fields lay sharply defined to the far horizon. Ponds and lakes gleamed like mirrors in the sun, and ruined villages lay here and there like the bones of long forgotten monsters. At intervals along the roads were long, black caterpillars that he knew were bodies of marching men, sometimes with wagons and artillery. There was nothing unusual about the scene, certainly nothing to cause the look of distaste on the pilot's face. It was an everyday scene on the Western Front.

The truth of the matter was he was setting out on a task that he expected would be wearisome to the point of utter boredom. He had never been detailed for this particular job before, but he had heard a good deal about it, and nothing that was pleasant. The work in question was that known throughout the Royal Flying Corps by those two mystic syllables 'art obs'—in other words, artillery observation.

There were certain squadrons that did nothing else but this work—ranging the guns of our artillery on those of the enemy; sometimes, however, the target was an ammunition dump, a bridge, or a similar strategical point that the higher command decided must be destroyed.

It was by no means as simple as it might appear, and the crew of the machine told off for the task were expected to remain at their post until each gun of the battery for which it was working had scored a hit, after which, without altering the range, they might continue to fire shot after shot at the target until it was wiped out of existence.

If the pilot was lucky, or clever, and the battery for which he was spotting good at its work, the job might be finished in an hour—or it might take three hours; and during the whole of that period the artillery aeroplane would have to circle continuously over the same spot, itself a target for every archie battery within range, and the prey of every prowling enemy scout.

Whether the task was more monotonous for the pilot, who had to watch his own battery for the flash of the gun and then the target for the bursting shell, signalling its position by the Morse code, or for the observer, whose duty it was not to watch the ground (as might reasonably be supposed) but the sky around for danger while the pilot was engrossed in his work, is a matter of opinion.

In any case, Biggles neither knew nor cared, but of one thing he was certain; circling in the same spot for hours was neither amusing nor interesting. Hence the unusual expression on his face as he made his way eastwards towards the Lines, to find the British battery for which he was detailed, and the enemy battery which the British guns proposed to wipe out. This being his first attempt at art obs, he was by no means sure that he would be able to find either of them, and this may have been another reason he was not flying with his usual enthusiasm.

Now, in order that the operation known as art obs should be understood, a few words of explanation are necessary, although the procedure is quite simple once the idea has been grasped. Biggles, like all other R.F.C. officers, had been given a certain amount of instruction at his training school, but as he had hoped to be sent to a scout squadron, which never did this class of work, he had not concentrated on the instruction as much as he might have done.

Briefly, this was the programme, for which, as a general rule, wireless was used, although occasionally a system of Very lights was employed. Wireless, at the time of which we are speaking, was of a primitive nature. The pilot, by means of an aerial which he lowered below the machine, could only send messages; he could not receive them. The gunners, in order to convey a message to the pilot, had to lay out strips of white material in the form of letters. The target was considered to be the centre of an imaginary clock, twelve o'clock being due north. Six o'clock was therefore due south, and the other cardinal points in their relative positions. Imaginary rings drawn round the target were lettered A, B, C, D, E, and F. These were 50, 100, 200, 300, 400, and 500 yards away respectively.

When the gunners started work, if the first shell dropped, say, one hundred yards away and due north of the target, all the pilot had to do was to signal B 12. 'B' meant that the shell burst one hundred yards away, and the '12' meant at twelve o'clock on the imaginary clock face. Thus the gunners were able to mark on their map exactly where the shell had fallen, and were therefore able to adjust their gun for the next shot. As another example, a shell bursting three hundred yards to the right of the target would be signalled D 3, or three hundred yards away at three o'clock. In this way the pilot was saved the trouble of tapping out long messages.

Briefly, while the 'shoot', as it was called, was in progress, the pilot continued to correct the aim of the gunners until they scored a hit. The first gun was now ranged on the target. The second gun was ranged in the same way, and so it went on until every gun in the battery was ranged on the target. Then they fired a salvo (all guns together) which the pilot would signal 'mostly O.K.', and thereafter the battery would pump out shells as fast as it could until the enemy guns were put out of action.

This is what Biggles had to do.

Approaching the Line, he quickly picked out the battery of guns for which he was to act as the 'eyes', and after a rather longer search he found the enemy battery, neatly camouflaged, and quite oblivious to the treat in store for it. He reached for his buzzer, which was a small key on the inside of his cockpit, and sent out a series of letter Bs in the Morse code, meaning 'Are you receiving my signals?'

This was at once acknowledged by the battery, which put

out three strips of white cloth in the form of a letter K—the recognition signal.

Biggles was rather amused, not to say surprised, at this prompt response. It struck him as strange that by pressing a lever in the cockpit he could make people on the ground do things. In fact, it was rather fun. He reached for his buzzer again, and sent K Q, K Q, K Q, meaning 'Are you ready to fire?' (All signals were repeated three times) Biggles, of course, could not hear his own signals; they were sent out by wireless, which was picked up on a small receiving set at the battery's listening-post.

The white strips of cloth on the ground at once took the form of a letter L, meaning 'Ready.'

G—G—G, buzzed Biggles. G was the signal to fire. Instantly a gun flashed, and Biggles, who was becoming engrossed in his task, turned his machine, eyes seeking the distant objective to watch the shell burst.

'Hi!'

The shrill shout from Mark Way, his observer, made him jump. Mark was pointing. Falling like a meteor from the sky was an Albatros, silver with scarlet wing-tips. The sun flashed on the gleaming wings, turning them into streaks of fire, on the ends of which were two large black crosses.

Biggles frowned and waved his hand impatiently. 'Make him keep out of the way!' he yelled, and turned back to watch the shell burst. But he was too late. A faint cloud of white smoke was drifting across the landscape near the target, but it was already dispersing, so it was impossible to say just where the shell had burst.

'Dash it!' muttered Biggles, turning and feeling for his buzzer. 'Now I've got to do it again.' G—G—G, he signalled.

There was a moment's pause before the gun flashed again, the gunners possibly wondering why he had not registered their first shot. Biggles turned again towards the target, but before the shell exploded the chatter of a machine-gun made him look up quickly. The Albatros had fired a burst at them, swung up in a climbing turn, and was now coming back at them.

'You cock-eyed son of a coot!' Biggles roared at Mark, as he turned to meet the attack. At this rate the job would never be done. 'And I'll give you something to fling yourself about for, you interfering hound!' he growled at the approaching Albatros. Curiously, it did not occur to him that their lives were in any particular danger, a fact which reveals the confidence that was coming to him as a result of experience. He was not in the least afraid of a single German aeroplane. However, he had still much to learn.

His windscreen flew to pieces, and something whanged against his engine. Again the Hun pulled up in a wonderful zoom, twisting cunningly out of the hail of lead that Mark's gun spat at him. He levelled out, turned, and came at them again.

For the first time it dawned on Biggles that the man in the machine was no ordinary pilot; he was an artist, a man who knew just what he was doing. Further, he had obviously singled him out for destruction. Well, the battery would have to wait, that was all.

Biggles brought his machine round to face the new attack, pulling his nose up to give Mark the chance of a shot. But before he could fire, the Hun had swerved in an amazing fashion to some point behind them, and a steady stream of bullets began to rip through the wings of the British machine. Again Biggles turned swiftly—but the Hun was not there.

Rat-tat-tat-tat-tat—a stream of lead poured up from below, one of the bullets jarring against the root of the joystick with a jerk that flung it out of his hand.

'You artful swipe!' rasped Biggles, flinging the F.E. round in such a steep turn that Mark nearly went overboard.

'Sorry!' Biggles' lips formed the words, but he was pointing at the Hun, who had climbed up out of range, but was now coming down again like a thunderbolt, guns spurting long streams of flame. Mark was shooting, too, their bullets seeming to meet between the two machines. The Albatros came so close that Biggles could distinctly see the tappets of the other's engine working, and the pilot's face peering at them over the side of his cockpit. Then he swerved, and Biggles breathed a sigh of relief.

But he was congratulating himself too soon. The Albatros twisted like a hawk, dived, turned as he dived, and then came up at them like a rocket. To Biggles this manœuvre was so unexpected, so seemingly impossible, that he could hardly believe it, and he experienced a real spasm of fright. He no longer thought of the battery below; he knew he was fighting the battle of his life, his first real duel against a man who knew his job thoroughly.

During the next five minutes he learnt many things, things that were to stand him in good stead later on, and the fact that he escaped was due, not to his ability, but to a circumstance for which he was duly grateful. Twice he had made a break, in the hope of reaching the Lines. For during the combat, as was so often the case, the wind had blown them steadily over enemy country, but each time the enemy was there first, cutting off his escape. Mark had not been idle, but the wily German seldom gave him a fair chance for even a fleeting shot, much less a 'sitter'.

The Hun seemed to attack from all points of the compass at once. Biggles turned to face his aggressor in a new quarter—the fellow was always in the most unexpected quarter—and dived furiously at him; too furiously. He overshot, and, before he could turn, the Hun was behind him, pouring hot lead into his engine.

He knew that he was lost. Something grazed his arm, and with horror he saw blood running down Mark's face. He crouched low as he tried to turn out of the hail of lead. The bullets stopped abruptly as he came round, glaring wildly. The Hun had gone. Presently Biggles made him out, dropping like a stone towards the safety of his own territory. He could hardly believe his eyes. He had been 'cold meat' for the enemy pilot, and he knew it. Why, then—— But Mark was pointing upwards, grinning.

Biggles' eyes followed the outstretched finger, and he saw a formation of nine Sopwith Pups sweeping across the sky five thousand feet above them. He grinned back, trembling slightly from reaction.

'By gosh, that was a close one! I'll remember that piece

of silver-and-red furniture, and keep out of his way!' he vowed, inwardly marvelling, and wondering how the Boche pilot had been able to concentrate his attack on him in the way that he had, and yet watch the surrounding sky for possible danger. He knew that if there had been a thousand machines in the sky he would not have seen them, yet the Hun had not failed to see the approaching Pups when they were miles away. 'Pretty good!' he muttered admiringly. 'I'll remember that!'

And he did. It was his first real lesson in the art of air combat. His pride suffered when he thought of the way the Hun had 'made rings round him,' and he was not quite as confident of himself as he had been, yet he knew that the experience was worth all the anxiety it had caused him.

But what about the enemy battery? He looked down, and saw that he had drifted miles away from it.

He snorted his disgust at the archie that opened up on him the instant the Hun had departed, and made his way back to his original rendezvous. The calico 'L' was still lying on the ground near the battery. Although he did not know it, the gunners had watched the combat with the greatest interest, and were agreeably surprised to see him returning so soon after the attack.

G—G—G—, he buzzed. The gun flashed, and the F.E. rocked suddenly, almost as if it had been shaken by an invisible hand.

Biggles started, and looked at his altimeter. In the fight he had, as usual, lost height, and he was now below three thousand feet. He knew that the great howitzer shell had passed close to him, so he started climbing as quickly as possible to get above its culminating point. The archie smoke was so thick that he had great difficulty in seeing the shell burst. It was a good five hundred yards short. F6 —F6—F6 he signalled; and then, after a brief interval: G—G—G—. He watched with interest for the next shell to burst, but it was farther from the mark than the first one had been.

'If they don't improve faster than that we shall still be

90

here when the bugles blow "Cease fire!"'" he muttered in disgust.

The next shot was better, but it was a good four hundred yards beyond the mark and slightly to the right. D1—D1—D1 he tapped out as he turned in a wide circle and then back again towards the target on a course which, had he been a sky-writer, would have traced a large figure eight— the usual method of the artillery spotting 'plane, which allowed the pilot to see both his own battery and the target in turn. It also kept the archie gunners guessing which way he was going next.

An hour later Biggles was still at it, and the first gun had got no closer than two hundred yards to its mark. The fascination of the pastime was beginning to wear off; indeed it was already bordering on the monotonous. 'This is a nice game played slow,' he shouted. 'Why don't those fellows learn to shoot?'

He was falling into a sort of reverie, sending his signals automatically, when he was again brought back to realities by a yell from Mark. He looked round sharply, and fixed his eyes on a small, straight-winged machine that was climbing up towards them from the east. The German anti-aircraft gunners must have seen it, too, for the archie died away abruptly as they ceased fire rather than take the risk of hitting their own man. There was no mistaking the machine. It was the red-and-silver Albatros.

Biggles was not to be caught napping twice. He turned his nose towards home and dived, only pulling out when he felt he was a safe distance over the Lines. He turned in time to see his late adversary gliding away into a haze that was forming over the other side of the Lines.

Once more he returned to his post, and signalled to the gunners to fire, but even as the gun flashed, he heard the *rat-tat-tat-tat* of a machine-gun, and the disconcerting *flac-flac-flac* of bullets ripping through his wings.

'You cunning hound!' he grated, seething with rage as he caught a glimpse of the red-and-silver wings of his old adversary as it darted in from the edge of the haze in which it had taken cover. It was another tip in the art of stalking that he did not forget. At the moment he was con-

91

cerned only with the destruction of his persistent tormentor, and he attacked with a fury that he had never felt before. He wanted to see the Albatros crash—he wanted to see that more than he had ever wanted to see anything in his life. Completely mastered by his anger, he made no attempt to escape, but positively flung the F.E. at the black-crossed machine. This was evidently something the Hun did not expect, and he was nearly caught napping.

Mark got in a good burst before the Hun swerved out of his line of fire. Biggles yanked the F.E. round in a turn that might have torn its wings off, and plunged down on the tail of the Albatros. He saw the pilot look back over his shoulder, and felt a curious intuition as to which way he would turn. He saw the Hun's rudder start to move, which confirmed it, and, without waiting for the Albatros actually to answer to its control, he whipped the F.E. round in a vertical bank.

The Hun had turned the same way, as he knew he must, and he was still on its tail, less than fifty yards away. It was a brilliant move, although at the time he did not know it; it showed anticipation in the moves of the game that marked the expert in air combat. He thrust the stick forward with both hands until he could see the dark gases flowing out of his enemy's exhaust-pipe; saw the pilot's blond moustache, saw the goggled eyes staring at him, and saw Mark's bullets sewing a leaden seam across his fuselage.

The Hun turned over on to its back and then spun, Biggles watching it with savage satisfaction that turned to chagrin when, a thousand feet from the ground, the red-and-silver machine levelled out and sped towards home. The pilot had deliberately thrown his machine out of order to mislead his enemy—another trick Biggles never forgot.

'We've given the blighter something to think about, at any rate!' he thought moodily, as he turned to the battery.

The gunners were waiting for him, but, to his annoyance and disgust, the first shot went wide; it was, in fact, farther away from the target than the first one had been.

'This is a game for mugs!' he snarled. 'As far as I can

see, there's nothing to prevent this going on for ever. Don't those fellows ever hit what they shoot at?'

He was getting tired, for they had now been in the air for more than three hours, and, as far as he could see, they were no nearer the end than when they started. The archie was getting troublesome again, and he was almost in despair when an idea struck him.

'H.Q. want that Hun battery blown up, do they?' he thought. 'All right, they shall have it blown up—but I know a quicker way of doing it than this.' He turned suddenly and raced back towards his aerodrome, sending the C H I signal as he went. C H I in the code meant 'I'm going home.' He landed and taxied up to the hangars.

'Fill her up with petrol and hang two 112-pounder bombs on the racks—and make it snappy!' he told the flight-sergeant. Then he hurried down to the mess and called up on the telephone the battery for which he had been acting.

'Look here,' he began hotly, 'I'm getting tired, trying to put you ham-fisted—What's that? Colonel? Sorry, sir!' He collected himself quickly, realizing that he had made a bad break. The brigade colonel was on the other end of the wire. 'Well, the fact is, sir,' he went on, 'I've just thought of an idea that may speed things up a bit. The target is a bit too low for you to see, I think, and—well, if I laid an egg on that spot it would show your gun-layers just where the target is. What's that, sir? Unusual? Yes, I know it is, but if it comes off it will save a lot of time and ammunition. If it fails I'll go on with the shoot again in the ordinary way. Yes, sir—very good, sir—I'll be over in about a quarter of an hour.'

He put the receiver down, and ignoring Toddy's cry of protest, hurried back to the sheds. Mark looked at him in astonishment when he climbed back into his seat. 'Haven't you had enough of it, or have you got a rush of blood to the brain?' he asked coldly.

'Brain, my foot!' snapped Biggles. 'I'm going to give those Huns a rush of something. I've done figures of eight until I'm dizzy. Round and round the blinking mulberry-bush, with archie battery for miles practising on me. I'm

93

going to liven things up a bit. You coming, or are you going to stay at home? Things are likely to get warmish.'

'Of course I'm coming!'

'Well, come on, let's get on with it.'

He took off, and climbed back to the old position between the batteries, but he sent no signal. He did not even let his aerial out. He began to circle as if he was going to continue the 'shoot,' but then, turning suddenly, he jammed his joy-stick forward with both hands and tore down at the German gunpits. For a few moments he left the storm of archie far behind, but as the gunners perceived his intention, it broke out again with renewed intensity, and the sky around him became an inferno of smoke and fire.

Crouching low in his cockpit, his lips pressed in a straight line, he did not swerve an inch. It was neck or nothing now, and he knew it. His only hope of success lay in speed. Any delay could only make his task more perilous, for already the artillery observers on the ground would be ringing up the *Jagdstaffeln* (German fighter squadrons), calling on them to deal with this Engländer who must either be mad or intoxicated.

He could see his objective clearly, and he made for it by the shortest possible course. Twice shells flamed so close to him that he felt certain the machine must fall in pieces out of his hands. The wind screamed in his wires and struts and plucked at his face and shoulders. A flying wire trailed uselessly from the root of an inter-plane strut, cut through as clean as a carrot by shrapnel, beating a wild tattoo on the fabric.

Mark was crouching low in the front cockpit, blood oozing from a flesh wound in his forehead, caused by flying glass.

It is difficult to keep track of time in such moments. The period from the start of his dive until he actually reached the objective was probably not more than three minutes—four at the most—but to Biggles it seemed an eternity. Time seemed to stand still; trifling incidents assumed enormous proportions, occurring as they did with slow deliberation. Thus, he saw a mobile archie battery, the gun mounted on a motor-lorry, tearing along the road. He saw it stop, and the well-trained team leap to their allotted stations; saw the long barrel swing round towards him, and the first flash of flame from its muzzle. He felt certain the shot would hit him, and wondered vaguely what the fellows at the squadron would say about his crazy exploit when he did not return.

The shell burst fifty feet in front of him, an orange spurt of flame that was instantly engulfed in a whirling ball of black smoke. He went straight through it, his propeller churning the smoke to the four winds, and he gasped as the acrid fumes bit into his lungs.

He saw the gun fire again, and felt the plunging machine lurch as the projectile passed desperately close. He did not look back, but he knew his track must be marked by a solid-looking plume of black smoke visible for miles. He wondered grimly what the colonel to whom he had spoken on the telephone was thinking about it, for he would be watching the proceedings.

Down—down—down, but there was no sensation of falling. The machine seemed to be stationary, with the earth rushing up to meet him. At five hundred feet the enemy gun-crew, who could not resist the temptation of watching him, bolted for their dug-outs like rabbits when a fox-terrier appears. Perhaps they had thought it impossible for the British machine to survive such a maelstrom of fire. Anyway, they left it rather late.

Not until he was within a hundred feet of the ground did Biggles start to pull the machine out of its dive, slowly, in case he stripped his wings off as they encountered the resistance of the air. Mark's gun was stuttering, bullets kicking up the earth about the gunpits in case one of the German gunners, bolder than the rest, decided to try his luck with a rifle or machine-gun.

The end came suddenly. Biggles saw the target leap towards him, and at what must have been less than fifty feet, he pulled his bomb toggle, letting both bombs go together. Then he zoomed high.

Such was his speed that he was back at a thousand feet when the two bombs burst simultaneously; but the blast of air lifted the F.E. like a piece of tissue paper. He fought

95

the machine back under control, and, without waiting to see the result of the explosion, tore in a zigzag course towards his own battery.

At three thousand feet he levelled out and looked back. He had succeeded beyond his wildest hopes, and knew that he must have hit the enemy ammunition dump. Flames were still leaping skyward in a dense pall of black smoke.

With a feeling of satisfaction, he lowered his aerial. His fingers sought the buzzer key and tapped out the letters G—G—G—. The British gun flashed instantly. The gun-layer was no longer firing blind, and the shot landed in the middle of the smoking mass.

O.K.—O.K.—O.K. tapped Biggles exultantly.

The second gun of the battery sent its projectile hurtling towards the Boche gunpits. It was less than one hundred yards short, but with a visible target to shoot at it required only two or three minutes to get it ranged on the target. The others followed.

G—D—O, G—D—O, G—D—O, tapped Biggles enthusiastically, for G—D—O was the signal to the gunners to begin firing in their own time. The four guns were ranged on the target, and they no longer needed his assistance. With salvo after salvo they pounded the enemy gunpits out of existence, Biggles and Mark watching the work of destruction with the satisfaction of knowing their job had been well done.

Then they looked at each other, and a slow smile spread over Biggles' face. C H I, C H I, C H I (I am going home) he tapped, and turned towards the aerodrome. Instantly his smile gave way to a frown of annoyance. What were the fools doing? A cloud of white archie smoke had appeared just in front of him. White archie!

Only British archie was white! Why were they shooting at him? The answer struck him at the same moment that Mark yelled and pointed. He lifted up his eyes. Straight across their front, in the direction they must go, but two thousand feet above them, a long line of white archie bursts trailed across the sky. In front of them, always it seemed just out of their reach, sped a small, straight-winged plane; its top wings were slightly longer than the lower ones.

Two thoughts rushed into Biggles' mind at once. The first was that the gunners on the ground had fired the burst to him to warn him of his danger, and the second was that the German machine was an Albatros. There was no mistaking the shark-like fuselage. Something, an instinct which he could not have explained, told him it was their old red-and-silver enemy. He was right—it was. At that moment it turned, and the sun revealed its colours. It dived towards the British machine, and the archie gunners were compelled to cease fire for fear of hitting the F.E.

There was no escape. Biggles would have avoided combat had it been possible, for he was rather worried about the damage the F.E. might have suffered during its dive. Mark glowered as he turned his gun towards the persistent enemy, and then crouched low, waiting for it to come into effective range.

But the Hun had no intention of making things so easy. His machine had already been badly knocked about in the last effort, an insult which he was probably anxious to avenge, and intended to see that no such thing occurred again. At two hundred feet he started shooting, and Biggles pulled his nose up to meet him. From that position he would not swerve, for it was a point of honour in the R.F.C. never to turn away from a frontal attack, even though the result was a collision.

Just what happened after that he was never quite sure. In trying to keep his nose on the Hun, who was still coming down from above, he got it too high up, with the result that one of two courses was open to him. Either he could let the F.E. stall, in which case the Hun would get a 'sitting' shot at him at the moment of stalling—a chance he was not likely to miss—or he could pull the machine right over in a loop. He chose the latter course.

As he came out of the loop, he looked round wildly for the Hun. For a fleeting fraction of an instant he saw him at his own level, not more than twenty or thirty feet away, going in the opposite direction. At the same moment he was nearly flung out of his seat by a jar that jerked him sideways and made the F.E. quiver from propeller boss to tail skid. His heart stood still, for he felt certain that his

97

top 'plane, or some other part of the machine, had broken away, but to his utter amazement it answered to the controls, and he soon had it on an even keel.

Mark was yelling, jabbing downwards with his finger. Biggles looked over the side of his cockpit. The Hun was gliding towards his own Lines.

There seemed to be something wrong with the Albatros—something missing; and for the moment Biggles could not make out what it was. Then he saw. It had no propeller! How the miracle had happened he did not know, and he had already turned to follow it to administer the knock-out when another yell from Mark made him change his mind—quickly. A formation of at least twenty Huns were tearing towards the scene.

Biggles waited for no more. He put his nose down for home and not until the aerodrome loomed upon the horizon did he ease the pace. He remembered his aerial, and took hold of the handle of the reel to wind in the long length of copper wire with its lead plummet on the end to keep it extended.

The reel was in place, but there was no aerial, and he guessed what had happened. He should have wound it in immediately he had sent C H I signal, and he knew that if he had done so he would in all probability by now be lying in a heap of charred wreckage in No Man's Land. He had forgotten to wind in, and to that fact he probably owed his life. When he had swung round after the loop, the wire, with the plummet on the end, must have swished round like a flail and struck the Boche machine, smashing its propeller!

The C.O. was waiting for them on the tarmac when they landed. There was a curious expression on his face, but several other officers who were standing behind him were smiling expectantly.

'You were detailed for the art obs show to-day, I think, Bigglesworth,' began Major Paynter coldly.

'That is so, sir,' said Biggles.

'Wing has just been on the telephone to me, and so has the commander of the battery for whom you were acting. Will you please tell me precisely what has happened?'

Briefly Biggles related what had occurred. The major did not move a muscle until he had finished. Then he looked at him with an expressionless face. 'Far be it from me to discourage zeal or initiative,' he said, 'but we cannot have this sort of thing. Your instructions were quite clear—you were to do the shoot for the artillery. You had no instructions to use bombs, and your action might have resulted in the loss of a valuable machine. I must discourage this excess of exuberance,' went on the C.O. 'As a punishment, you will return this afternoon to the scene of the affair, taking a camera with you. I shall require a photograph of the wrecked German battery on my desk by one hour after sunset. Is that clear?'

'Perfectly, sir.'

'That's all, then. Don't let it happen again. The artillery think we are trying to do them out of their jobs; but it was a jolly good show, all the same!' he concluded, with something as near a chuckle as his dignity would permit.

THERE WAS NO HURRY. Major Paynter, the C.O., had not named any particular hour for the 'show.' He had said that the photographs must be delivered to him by one hour after sunset and there were still five hours of daylight.

With Mark, Biggles made his way to the mess for a rest, and over coffee they learned some news that set every member of the squadron agog with excitement. Toddy, the Recording Officer, divulged that the equipment of the squadron was to be changed, the change to take effect as quickly as possible. In future they were to fly Bristol Fighters.

It transpired that Toddy had been aware of the impending change for some time, but the orders had been marked 'secret,' so he had not been allowed to make the information public. But now that ferry pilots were to start delivering the new machines, there was no longer any need to keep silent. They might expect the Bristols to arrive at any time, Toddy told them, and A Flight, by reason of its seniority, was to have the first.

Biggles, being in A Flight, was overjoyed. He had grown very attached to his old F.E. which had given him good service, but it had always been a source of irritation to him, as the pilot, that the actual shooting had perforce been left to Mark. In future they would both have guns, to say nothing of a machine of higher performance.

In the excitement caused by the news the time passed quickly, and it was nearly two-thirty when they walked towards the sheds in order to proceed with the work for which they had been detailed.

Biggles' shoulder had been grazed by a bullet in the

morning's combat with the red-and-silver Albatros, but it caused him no inconvenience, and he did not bother to report it. Neither had Mark's wound been very severe, not much more than a scratch, as he himself said, and it did not occur to him to go 'sick' with it. It was a clean cut in his forehead about an inch long, caused by a splinter of flying glass. He had washed it with antiseptic, stuck a piece of plaster over it, and dismissed it from his mind. On their way to the hangars they met the medical officer on his way back from visiting some mechanics who were sick in their huts. They were about to pass him with a cheerful nod when his eyes fell on the strip of court-plaster on Mark's forehead. He stopped and raised his eyebrows. 'Hallo, what have you been up to?' he asked.

'Up to?' echoed Mark, not understanding.

'What have you done to your head?'

'Oh—that! Nothing to speak of. I stopped a piece of loose glass in a little affair with a Hun this morning,' replied Mark casually.

'Let me have a look at it.' The M.O. removed the piece of court-plaster and examined the wound critically. 'Where are you off to now?' he inquired.

'I've got a short show to do with Bigglesworth.'

'Short or long, you'll do no more flying to-day, my boy; you get back to your quarters and rest for a bit. Too much cold air on that cut, and we shall have you down with erysipelas. I'll speak to the C.O.'

'But——' began Mark, in astonishment.

'There's no "but" about it,' said the M.O. tersely. 'You do as you're told, my lad. Twelve hours' rest will put you right. Off you go!'

Mark looked at Biggles hopelessly.

'Doc's right, Mark,' said Biggles, nodding. 'I ought to have had the sense to know it myself. I'll bet your skull aches even now.'

'Not it!' snorted Mark.

'That's all right, doc, I'll find another partner,' asserted Biggles. 'See you later, Mark.'

He made his way to the Squadron Office and reported the matter to Toddy.

'You wouldn't like to take one of the new fellows, I suppose?' suggested Toddy, referring to two new observer officers who had reported for duty the previous evening. 'I think they're about somewhere.'

'Certainly I will,' replied Biggles. 'Someone will have to take them over some time, so the sooner the better. It's only a short show, anyway.'

Toddy dispatched an orderly at the double to find the new officers, and Biggles awaited their arrival impatiently. He had already spoken to them, so they were not quite strangers, but they were of such opposite types that he could not make up his mind which one to choose. Harris was a mere lad, fair-haired and blue-eyed, straight from school. He had failed in his tests as a pilot, and was satisfied to take his chance as an aerial gunner rather than go into the infantry. Culver, the other, was an older man, a cavalry captain who had seen service in the Dardanelles before he had transferred to the R.F.C.

They came in quickly, anxious to know what was in the wind. Briefly, Biggles told them and explained the position. 'Toss for it,' he suggested. 'That's the fairest way. All I ask is that whoever comes will keep his eyes wide open and shoot straight, if there is any shooting to be done.'

Harris won the toss, and with difficulty concealed his satisfaction, for although Biggles was unaware of it, he— Biggles—had already achieved the reputation of being one of the best pilots in the squadron.

'Good enough. Get into your flying kit and get a good gun,' Biggles said shortly. 'I'll go and start up.'

He was satisfied but by no means enthusiastic about taking the new man. Few experienced pilots felt entirely happy in the company of men new to the job and who had not had an opportunity of proving themselves. It was not that cowardice was anticipated. Biggles knew what all experienced flyers knew; that a man could be as plucky as they make them when on the ground—might have shown himself to be a fearless fighter in trench warfare—but until he had been put to the test it was impossible to say how he would behave in his first air combat; how he would react to the terrifying sensation of hearing bullets ripping through spruce and canvas.

As a matter of fact, it was worse for an observer than it was for a pilot. It needed a peculiar kind of temperament, or courage, to stand up and face twin machine-guns spouting death at point-blank range; not only to stand up, but calmly align the sights of a Lewis gun and return the fire.

There was only one way to find out if a man could do it and that was to take him into the air. There were some who could not do it, in the same way that there were cases of officers who could not face 'archie.' And after one or two trips over the Lines this was apparent to others, even if it was not admitted. And it needed a certain amount of courage to confess. But it was better for an officer to be frank with his C.O. and tell the truth, rather than throw away his life, and an aeroplane. Officers reporting 'sick' in this way were either transferred to ground duties or sent home for instructional work.

Biggles wore a worried frown, therefore, as he walked up to the sheds. He realized for the first time just how much confidence he had in Mark, and the comfort he derived from the knowledge that he had a reliable man in the observer's cockpit.

They took their places in the machine, and after Biggles had given Harris a reassuring smile he took off and headed for the strafed German battery. He would gain all the height he needed on the way to the Lines, for he proposed to take the photographs from not higher than five thousand feet. A good deal of cloud had drifted up from the west, which was annoying, for it was likely to make his task more difficult. It would not prevent him reaching his objective, but the C.O. would certainly not be pleased if he was handed a nice photograph of a large white cloud.

He crossed the Lines at four thousand, still climbing, and zigzagged his way through the archie in the direction of the wrecked German battery. He noted with satisfaction that his new partner took his baptism of anti-aircraft fire well, for he turned and smiled cheerfully, even if the smile was a trifle forced. He was rather pale, but Biggles paid no attention to that. There are few men who do not change colour the first time they find themselves under fire.

The sky seemed clear of aircraft, although the cloud formed good cover for lurking enemy scouts, and he began to hope the job might be done in record time. He skirted a massive pile of cloud, and there, straight before him, lay the scene of his morning exploit. A grin spread over his face as he surveyed the huge craters that marked the spot where the enemy battery had once hidden itself; the job had been done thoroughly, and headquarters could hardly fail to be pleased.

After a swift glance around he put his nose down and dived, and then, swinging upwind, he began to expose his plates. In five minutes he had been over the whole area twice, covering not only the actual site of the battery, but the surrounding country. With the satisfaction of knowing that his job had been well done, he turned for home. 'Good!' he muttered. 'That's that!'

Swinging round another towering mass of opaque mist he ran into a one-sided dog-fight with a suddenness that almost caught him off his guard. A lone F.E. was fighting a battle with five enemy Albatroses.

Now, according to the rules of war flying, this was no affair of Biggles'. Strictly speaking, the duty of a pilot with a definite mission was to fulfil that mission and return home as quickly as possible; but, needless to say, this was not always adhered to. Few pilots could resist the temptation of butting into a dog-fight, or attacking an enemy machine if one was seen. To leave a comrade fighting overwhelming odds was unthinkable.

Biggles certainly did not think about it. The combat was going on at about his own altitude, and although the F.E. had more than one opportunity of dodging into the clouds and thereby escaping, the pilot had obviously made up his mind to see the matter through.

Biggles' lips parted in a smile and he barged into the fight. Then, to his horror, he saw that his gunner was not even looking at the milling machines. He had not even seen them. It seemed incredible. But there it was. And Biggles, remembering his own blindness when he was a beginner, forgave him. Harris was gazing at the ground immediately below with an almost bored expression on his face.

'Hi!' roared Biggles, with the full power of his lungs. 'Get busy!'

Harris' start of astonishment and horror as he looked up just as a blue Albatros dashed across his nose was almost comical; but he grabbed his gun like lightning and sent stream of lead after the whirling Hun.

Biggles dashed in close to the other F.E. to make his presence known. A swift signal greeting passed between the two pilots, and then they set about the work on hand.

The fight did not last many minutes, but it was red-hot while it lasted. One Albatros went down in flames; another glided down out of control with its engine evidently out of action. The other three dived for home. Biggles straightened his machine and looked around for the other F.E., but it had disappeared. He had not seen it go, so whether it had been shot down, or had merely proceeded on its way, he was unable to ascertain.

Harris was standing up surveying their own machine ruefully, for it had been badly shot about. Biggles caught his eye and nodded approvingly. 'You'll do!' he told himself; for the boy had undoubtedly acquitted himself well. Then he continued on his course for the aerodrome.

He reached it without further incident and taxied in, eyes on a brand new Bristol Fighter that was standing on the tarmac. The photographic sergeant hurried towards him to collect the camera and plates, in order to develop them forthwith. Biggles jumped to the ground, and was about to join the group of officers admiring the Bristol when a cry from the N.C.O. made him turn.

'What's the matter?' he asked quickly.

'Sorry, sir, but look!' said the sergeant apologetically.

Biggles' eyes opened wide as they followed the N.C.O.'s pointing finger, and then he made a gesture of anger and disgust. The camera was bent all shapes, and the plate container was a perforated wreck. There was no need to wonder how it had happened; a burst of fire from one of the enemy machines had reduced the camera to a twisted ruin.

He could see at a glance that the plates were spoilt. His

105

journey had been in vain. Looking over the machine thoroughly for the first time he saw that the damage was a good deal worse than he had thought. Two wires had been severed and one of the hinges of his elevators shot off. The machine had brought him home safely, but in its present condition it was certainly not safe to fly.

'What's the matter?' asked Mapleton, his flight-commander, seeing that something was wrong.

Briefly, Biggles explained the catastrophe.

'What are you going to do about it?' asked Mabs.

'I'll have to do the show again, that's all about it!' replied Biggles disgustedly. 'The Old Man was very decent about this morning's effort. He's waiting for these photos; I can't let him down.'

'You can't fly that machine again to-day, that's a certainty.'

'So I see.'

'Would you like to try the Bristol?'

Biggles started. 'I'd say I would!'

'You can have it if you like, but for the love of Mike don't hurt it. It's been allotted to me, so it's my pigeon. She's all O.K. and in fighting trim. I was just off to try her out myself.'

'That's jolly sporting of you,' declared Biggles. 'I shan't be long, and I'll take care of her. Come on, Harris, get your guns—and get me another camera, sergeant; look sharp, it will soon be dark.'

In a few minutes Biggles was in the air again, on his way to the enemy battery for the third time that day. He had no difficulty in flying the Bristol, which was an easy machine to fly, and after a few practice turns he felt quite at home in it.

He noticed with dismay that the clouds were thickening, and he was afraid that they might totally obscure the objective. Twice, as he approached it, he thought he caught sight of a lurking shadow, dodging through the heavy cloud-bank above him, but each time he looked it had vanished before he could make sure.

'There's a Hun up there, watching me, or I'm a Dutchman,' he mused uneasily. 'I hope that kid in the back

106

seat will keep his eyes skinned.' He shot through a small patch of cloud and distinctly saw another machine disappear into a cloud just ahead and above him. It was an Albatros, painted red and silver. 'So it's you, is it?' he muttered, frowning, for the idea of taking on his old antagonist with a comparatively untried gunner in the back seat did not fill him with enthusiasm. With Mark it would have been a different matter.

He turned sharply into another cloud and approached the objective on a zigzag course, never flying straight for more than a few moments at a time. He knew that this would leave the watcher, if he were still watching, in doubt as to his actual course, but it was nervy work, knowing that an attack might be launched at any moment.

As he expected, he found the battery concealed under a thick layer of grey cloud, but he throttled back and came out below it at two thousand feet. Instantly he was the target for a dozen archie batteries, but he ignored them and flew level until he had exposed all his plates. He was feeling more anxious than he had ever felt before in the air, not so much for his own safety as for the safety of Mab's machine, so it was with something like a sigh of relief that he finished his task, jammed the throttle wide open, and zoomed upwards through the opaque ceiling.

The instant he cleared the top side of the cloud the rattle of a machine-gun came to his ears and the Bristol quivered as a stream of lead ripped through it. He whirled round just in time to see the red-and-silver 'plane zoom over him, not twenty feet away. Why hadn't Harris fired? Was he asleep, the young fool? With his brow black as thunder Biggles twisted round in his seat and looked behind him. Harris was lying in a crumpled heap on the side of his cockpit.

Biggles went ice-cold all over. The corners of his mouth turned down. 'He's got him!' he breathed, and then exposing his teeth, 'You hound!' he grated, and dragged the Bristol round on its axis and in the direction of the Albatros, now circling to renew the attack.

If the Boche pilot supposed that the British machine would now seek to escape he was mistaken. Unknowingly, he was faced with the most dangerous of all opponents, a pilot who was fighting mad. A clever, calculating enemy, fighting in cold blood, was a foe to be respected; but a pilot seeing red and seething with hate was much worse. For the first time, the war had become a personal matter with Biggles, and he would have rammed his adversary if he could have reached him.

The pilot in the black-crossed machine seemed to realize this, for he suddenly broke off the combat and sought to escape by diving towards the nearest cloud. Biggles was behind him in a flash, eye to the Aldis sight. Farther and yet farther forward he pushed the control-stick, and the distance rapidly closed between them.

The Hun saw death on his tail and twisted like an eel, but the Bristol stuck to him as if connected by an invisible wire. A hundred feet—fifty feet—Biggles drew nearer, but still he did not fire. The glittering arc of his propeller was nearly touching the other's elevators. The cross-wire of the Aldis sight cut across the tail, crept along the fuselage to the brown-helmeted head in the cockpit.

Biggles knew that he had won and was filled with a savage exultation. He was so close that every detail of the Boche machine was indelibly imprinted on his brain. He could see the tappets of the Mercedes engine working, and the dark smoke pouring from its exhaust. He could even see the patches over the old bullet holes in the lower wings. His gloved hand sought the Bowden lever, closed on it, and gripped it hard. Orange flame darted from the muzzle of his gun and the harsh metallic clatter of the cocking handle filled his ears. The Albatros jerked upwards, the Bristol still on its tail. A tongue of scarlet flame licked along its side, and a cloud of black smoke poured out of the engine. The pilot covered his face with his hands.

Biggles turned away, feeling suddenly limp. He seemed to have awakened with a shock from a vivid dream. Where was he? He did not know. He saw the Hun break up just as it reached the lower stratum of cloud, and he followed it down to try to pick up some landmark that would give him his position. It was with real relief that he was able to recognize the road near where the wreck of the Albatros had fallen, and he shot upwards again to escape the ever-present archie.

For the first time since the fight began he remembered Harris, and raced for home. He tried to persuade himself that perhaps he was only wounded, but in his heart of hearts he knew the truth. Harris was dead. Four straight-winged 'planes materialized out of the mist in front of him, but Biggles did not swerve. The feeling of hate began to surge through him again. 'If you're looking for trouble you can have it!' he snarled, and tore straight at the Alba-troses.

They opened up to let him go through, and then closed in behind him. He swerved round a fragment of cloud, and then, with the speed of light, flung the Bristol on its side with a sharp intake of breath. It was perhaps only because his nerves were screwed up to snapping point that he had caught sight of what seemed to be a fine wire standing vertically in the air.

Without even thinking, he knew it was a balloon cable. Somewhere above the clouds an enemy observation bal-loon was taking a last look round the landscape, or as much of it as could be seen, before being wound down for the night. Then an idea struck him, and he swerved in the opposite direction.

The leading Hun, with his eyes only on the Bristol was round in a flash to cut across the arc of the circle and intercept him, and Biggles witnessed just what he hoped would happen—the picture of a machine colliding with a balloon cable. It was a sight permitted to very few war pilots, although it actually happened several times.

The cable tore the top and bottom port wings off the Albatros as cleanly as if they had been sheared through with an axe. The machine swung round in its own length, and the pilot was flung clean over the centre section. He fell, clutching wildly at space. Biggles saw that the cable had parted, and that the other machines were hesitating, watching their falling leader. Then they came on again. They overtook him before he reached the Lines, as he knew they would. A bullet splashed into his instrument-board, and he had no alternative but to turn and face them.

With a steady gunner in the back seat he would have felt no qualms as to the ultimate result of the combat, but with his rear gun silent he was much worse off than the single-seaters, as he had a larger machine to handle. To make matters worse, the Lewis gun, pointing up to the sky in the rear cockpit, told its own story. The enemy pilots knew that his gunner was down, and that they could get on his tail with impunity.

The three Boche pilots were evidently old hands, for they separated and then launched an attack from three directions simultaneously. The best that Biggles could do was to take on one machine at a time, yet while he was engaging it his flanks and tail were exposed to the attacks of the other two.

Several bullets struck the Bristol, and it began to look as if his luck had broken at last. He fought coolly, without the all-devouring hate that had consumed him when he attacked the red-and-silver Albatros. These methods would not serve him now.

He tried to break out of the circle into which they had automatically fallen in order to reach the shelter of the clouds, but a devastating blast of lead through his centre section warned him of the folly of turning his back on them. He swung round again to meet them. A shark-like aircraft, painted dark green and buff, circled to get behind him; the other two were coming in from either side. His position, he knew, was critical.

Then a miracle happened, or so it seemed. The circling Hun broke into pieces and hurtled earthwards. Biggles stared, and then understood. A drab-coloured single-seater, wearing red, white, and blue ring markings, swept across his nose. It was a Sopwith Pup. He looked around quickly for others, but it was alone.

Its advent soon decided matters. The black-crossed machines dived out of the fight and disappeared into the clouds. Biggles waved his hand to the single-seater pilot and they turned towards the Lines. The Pup stayed with him until the aerodrome loomed up through the gloom, and then disappeared as magically as it had arrived.

Biggles felt for his Very pistol and fired a red light over

the side. The ruddy glow cast a weird light over the twilight scene. He saw the ambulance start out almost before his wheels had touched the ground, and he taxied to meet it. Mabs and Mark were following it at a brisk trot; the C.O. was standing in the doorway of the squadron office.

Mark, with a bandage round his head, caught Biggles' eye as two R.A.M.C. men gently lifted the dead observer from his seat. Biggles did not look; he felt that tears were not far away, and was ashamed of his weakness. He taxied up to the sheds and climbed wearily to the ground.

'How did the Bristol go?' asked Mabs awkwardly.

'Bristol? Oh, yes——fine, thanks!'

The photographic sergeant removed the camera.

'See that the prints are in the squadron office as quickly as you can manage it,' Biggles told him.

'Lucky for me the doc made me stay at home,' observed Mark.

Biggles shrugged his shoulders. 'Maybe. On the other hand, it might not have happened if you'd been there.'

'How did it happen?' asked the C.O., coming up.

Briefly Biggles told him.

'Anyway, it's some consolation that you got the Hun,' said the C.O.

'Yes, I got him!' answered Biggles grimly.

'And the photos?'

'You'll have them in time, sir.'

'Cheer up,' whispered Mark, as they walked slowly towards the mess. 'It's a beastly business, but it's no good getting down-hearted.'

'I know,' replied Biggles. 'It's the sort of thing that's liable to happen to any of us—will happen, I expect, before we're very much older. But it was tough luck for Harris. He'd only been here about five minutes, and now he's gone—gone before he fully realized what he was up against. It's ghastly.'

'It's war!' retorted Mark. 'Try to forget it, or we'll have you getting nervy. The other Bristols will be here in the morning,' he added, changing the subject.

'Mahoney, of 266, is on the 'phone asking for you,' shouted Toddy, as they passed the squadron office. 'He asked me who was in the Bristol, and when I told him it was you he said he'd like to have a word with you.'

Biggles picked up the receiver. 'Hallo, Mahoney!' he said.

'You'll be saying hallo to the Flanders poppies if you don't watch your step, my lad!' Mahoney told him seriously.

Biggles started. 'What do you know about it?' he asked quickly.

'Know about it? I like that,' growled Mahoney, over the wire. 'Is that all the thanks I get——?'

'Was that you in the Pup?' interrupted Biggles, suddenly understanding.

'What other fool do you suppose would risk being fried alive to get a crazy Bristol out of a hole? You ought to look where you're going. Have you bought the sky, or something?'

'Why, have you sold it?' asked Biggles naïvely.

There was a choking noise at the other end of the wire. Then: 'You watch your step, laddie! We want you in 266. The Old Man has already sent in an application for your transfer, but it looks to me as if he's wasted his time. You'll be cold meat before——'

'Oh, rats!' grinned Biggles. 'I'm just beginning to learn something about this game. You watch your perishing Pup!'

'Well, we're quits now, anyway,' observed Mahoney.

'That's as it should be,' replied Biggles. 'Meet me to-night in the town and I'll stand you a dinner on the strength of it.'

'I'll be there!' Mahoney told him briskly. 'Bring your wallet—you'll need it!'

The 'Show'

BIGGLES HAD JUST left the fireside circle preparatory to going to bed when Major Paynter entered the officers' mess.

'Pay attention, everybody, please!' said the major, rather unnecessarily, for an expectant hush had fallen on the room. 'A big attack along this entire section of Front has been planned to come into operation in the near future. If weather conditions permit, it may start to-morrow morning. As far as this squadron is concerned, every available machine will leave the ground at dawn, and, flying as low as possible, harass the enemy's troops within the boundaries you'll find marked on the large map in the squadron office. Each machine will carry eight Cooper bombs and work independently, concentrating on preventing the movement of enemy troops on the roads leading to the Front. Every officer will do three patrols of two and a half hours each daily, until further notice.

'The greatest care must be exercised in order that pilots and observers do not fire on our own troops, who will disclose their positions, as far as they are able, with Very lights and ground strips. Their objective is the high ridge which at present runs about two miles in front of our forward positions. These are the orders, gentlemen. I understand that all British machines not actually engaged in ground strafing will be in the air, either bombing back areas or protecting the low-flying machines from air attack. I need hardly say that the higher command relies implicitly on every officer carrying out his duty to the best possible advantage; the impending battle may have very decisive results on the progress of the War. I think that's all. All previous orders are cancelled. Officers will muster on the tarmac at six-fifty, by which time it should be light enough to see to take off. Good night, everybody.'

A babble of voices broke out as the C.O. left the mess.

'That's the stuff!' declared Mark Way, enthusiastically

Mabs eyed him coldly. 'Have you done any trench strafing?' he asked. 'I don't mean just emptying your guns into the Lines as you come back from an O.P.,* but as a regular job during one of these big offensives?'

Mark shook his head. 'As a matter of fact, I haven't,' he admitted.

Mabs grinned sarcastically. 'Inside three days you'll be staggering about looking for somewhere to sleep. But there won't be any sleep. You're going to know what hard work is for the first time in your life. I was in the big spring offensive last year, and the Hun counter-attack that followed it, and by the time it was over I never wanted to see another aeroplane again as long as I lived. You heard what the Old Man said—three shows a day. By this time to-morrow you won't be able to see the ground for crashes, and those that can still fly will have to do the work of the others as well as their own.'

'You're a nice cheerful cove, I must say!' said Biggles.

'Well, you might as well know what we're in for,' returned Mabs, 'and it won't come as a surprise! When you've flown up and down a double artillery barrage for a couple of hours you'll know what flying is.' He rose and made for the door. 'I'm going to hit the sheets,' he announced. 'Get to bed, officers of A Flight, please. It may be the last chance you'll get for some time!'

There was a general move towards the door as he disappeared.

'Tired or not, I've got an appointment with a steak and chips in Rouen to-morrow night,' declared Curtiss, of B Flight, yawning, little dreaming that he was going to bed for the last time in his life.

The tarmac, just before daybreak the following morning, was a scene of intense activity. Nine big, drab-coloured Bristol Fighters stood in line in front of the flight sheds,

* Offensive Patrol

with a swarm of air mechanics bustling about them, adjusting equipment and fitting Cooper bombs on the bomb racks. Propellers were being turned round and engines started up, while the *rat-tat-tat-tat* of machine-guns came from the direction of the gun-testing pits. Biggles' fitter was standing by his machine.

'Everything all right?' asked Biggles.

'All ready, sir,' was the reply.

'Suck in, then!' called Biggles, as he climbed into his cockpit. 'Suck in' was the signal to suck petrol into the cylinders of the engine.

Mark, his gunner, disappeared for a few moments, to return with a Lewis gun, which he adjusted on the Scarff mounting round the rear seat. A mechanic handed up a dozen drums of ammunition.

The engine roared into pulsating life, and Biggles fixed his cap and goggles securely as he allowed it to warm up. Mabs' machine, wearing streamers on wing-tips and tail, began to taxi out into position to take off. The others followed. For a minute or two they waddled across the soaking turf like a flock of ungainly geese. Then, with a roar that filled the heavens, they skimmed into the air and headed towards the Lines. They kept no particular formation, but generally followed the direction set by the leader. The work before them did not call for close formation flying.

A watery sun, still low on the eastern horizon, cast a feeble and uncertain light over the landscape, the British reserve trenches, and the war-scarred battlefields beyond. Patches of ground mist still hung here and there towards the west, but for the most part the ground lay fairly clear. Signs of the activity on the ground were at once apparent. Long lines of marching men, guns, horses, and ammunition wagons were winding like long grey caterpillars towards the Front. A group of queer-looking toad-like monsters slid ponderously over the mud, and Biggles watched them for a moment with interest. He knew they were tanks, the latest engines of destruction.

The ground was dull green, with big bare patches, pockmarked with holes, some of which were still smoking, showing where shells had recently fallen. A clump of shattered trees, blasted into bare, gaunt spectres, marked the site of what had once been a wood. Straight ahead, the green merged into a dull brown sea of mud, flat except for the craters and shell-holes, marked with countless zigzag lines of trenches in which a million men were crouching in readiness for the coming struggle.

Beyond the patch of barren mud the green started again, dotted here and there with roofless houses and shattered villages. In the far distance a river wound like a gleaming silver thread towards the horizon. Spouting columns of flame and clouds of smoke began to appear in the sea of mud; the brown earth was flung high into the air by the bursting shells.

It was a depressing sight, and Biggles, turning his eyes upwards, made out a number of black specks against the pale blue sky. They were the escorting scouts. In one place a dog-fight was raging, and he longed to join in it, but the duty on hand forbade it. He nestled a little lower in his cockpit, for the air was cold and damp, so cold that his fingers inside the thick gauntlets were numbed. They had nearly reached the Lines now, so he turned his eyes to Mabs' machine, watching for the signal Very light that would announce the attack. It came, a streak of scarlet flame that described a wide parabola before it began to drop earthwards Simultaneously the machine from which it had appeared roared down towards the ground. The open formation broke up as each pilot selected his own target and followed.

Biggles saw the welter of mud leaping up at him as he thrust the control-stick forward, eyes probing the barren earth for the enemy. Guns flashed like twinkling stars in all directions. He saw a Pup, racing low, plunge nose-first into the ground to be swallowed up by an inferno of fire.

Charred skeletons of machines lay everywhere, whether friend or foe it was impossible to tell. Lines of white tracer bullets streamed upwards, seeming to move quite slowly. Something smashed against the engine cowling of the Bristol and Biggles ducked instinctively.

Rat-tat-tat-tat-tat! Mark's gun began its staccato chatter, but Biggles did not look round to see what he was shooting at; his eyes were on the ground. The sky above would have to take care of itself. The needle of his altimeter was falling steadily; five hundred feet, four hundred, yet he forced it lower, throttle wide open, until the ground flashed past at incredible speed.

He could hear the guns now, a low rumble that reminded him of distant thunder on a summer's day. He heard bullets ripping through the machine somewhere behind him, and kicked hard on right rudder, swerving farther into enemy country. He could still see Mabs' machine some distance ahead and to the left of him, nose tilted down to the ground, a stream of tracer bullets pouring from the forward gun.

Something tapped him sharply on the shoulder and he looked round in alarm. Mark was pointing. Following the outstretched finger he picked out a mud-churned road. A long column of troops in field-grey were marching along it, followed by guns or wagons, he could not tell which.

He swung the Bristol round in its own length, noting with a curious sense of detachment that had he continued flying on his original course for another two seconds the machine must have been blown to smithereens, for a jagged sheet of flame split the air; it was too large for an ordinary archie and must have been a shell from a field-gun. Even as it was, the Bristol bucked like a wild horse in the blast.

He tilted his nose down towards the German infantry and watched them over the top of his engine cowling. His hand sought the bomb-toggle. There was a rending clatter as a stream of machine-gun bullets made a colander of his right wing; a wire snapped with a sharp twang, but he did not alter his course.

A cloud of smoke, mixed with lumps of earth, shot high into the air not fifty yards away, and again the machine rocked. He knew that any second might be his last, but the thought did not worry him. Something at the back of his mind seemed to be saying: 'This is war, war, war!' and he hated it. This was not his idea of flying; it was just a welter of death and destruction.

The enemy troops were less than five hundred yards

117

away, and he saw the leaders pointing their rifles at him. He drew level with the head of the column, and jerked the bomb-toggle savagely. Then he kicked the rudder-bar hard, and at the same time jerked the control-stick back; even so, he was nearly turned upside-down by the force of the explosions, and clods of earth and stones dropped past him from above.

He glanced down. The earth was hidden under a great cloud of smoke. Again he swept down, tore straight along the road, and released the remainder of his bombs. Again he zoomed upwards.

The air was filled with strange noises; the crash of bursting shells, the clatter of his broken wire beating against a strut, and the slap-slap-slap of torn fabric on his wings. Mark's gun was still chattering, which relieved him, for it told him that all was still well with his partner. He half-turned and glanced back at the place where he had dropped his bombs.

There were eight large, smoking holes, around which a number of figures were lying; others were running away. It struck him that he was some way over the Lines, so he turned again and raced back towards the conspicuous stretch of No Man's Land, across which figures were now hurrying at a clumsy run. Nearer to him a number of grey-coated troops were clustered around a gun, and he sprayed them with a shower of lead as he passed.

He reached the Line, and raced along it, keeping well over the German side to make sure of not hitting any British troops who might have advanced. Burst after burst he poured into the trenches and at the concrete pill-boxes in which machine-guns nestled.

He passed a Bristol lying upside-down on the ground, and a scout seemingly undamaged. Mark tapped him on the shoulder, turned his thumbs down and pointed to his gun, and Biggles knew that he meant that his ammunition was finished.

'I'll finish mine, too, and get out of this!' he thought. 'I've had enough.' He took sights on a group of men who were struggling to drag a field-gun to the rear, and they flung themselves flat as the withering hail smote them.

Biggles held the Bowden lever of his gun down until the gun ceased firing, then turned and raced towards his own side of the Lines.

Some Tommies waved to him as he skimmed along not fifty feet above their heads. Mark returned the salutation. The Bristol rocked as it crossed the tracks of heavy shells, and Biggles breathed a sigh of relief as they left the war zone behind them.

Five machines, one of which was Mabs', had already returned when they landed, their crews standing about on the tarmac discussing the 'show.'

'Well, what do you think of it?' asked the flight-commander as Biggles and Mark joined them.

'Rotten!' replied Biggles, buffing his arms to restore circulation. He felt curiously exhausted, and began to understand the strain that low flying entails.

'Get filled up, and then rest while you can. We leave the ground again in an hour!' Mabs told them. 'The enemy are giving way all along the sector and we've got to prevent them bringing up reinforcements.'

'I see,' replied Biggles, without enthusiasm. 'In that case we might as well go down to the mess. Come on, Mark.'

FOR THREE DAYS the attack continued. The squadron lost four machines; two others were unserviceable. The remainder were doing four shows a day, and Biggles staggered about almost asleep on his feet. Life had become a nightmare. Even when he flung himself on his bed at night he could not sleep. In his ears rang the incessant roar of his engine, and his bed seemed to stagger in the bumps of bursting shells, just as the Bristol had done during the day. Mabs had gone to hospital with a bullet through the leg, and new pilots were arriving to replace casualties.

On the fourth morning he made his way, weary and unrefreshed to the sheds; Mark, who was also feeling the strain, had preceded him. They seldom spoke. They no longer smiled. Mark eyed him grimly as he reached the Bristol and prepared to climb into his seat. 'Why so pale and wan, young airman, prithee why so pale?' he misquoted mockingly.

Biggles looked at him coldly. 'I'm sick and I'm tired,' he said, 'and I've got a nasty feeling that our turn is about due. Just a hunch that something's going to happen, that's all,' he concluded shortly.

'You'll make a good undertaker's clerk when this is over, you cheerful Jonah!' growled Mark.

'Well, come on, let's get on with it. Personally, I'm beyond caring what happens,' replied Biggles, climbing into his seat.

He was thoroughly sick of the war; the futility of it appalled him. He envied the scouts circling high in the sky as they protected the low-flying trench strafers; they were putting in long hours, he knew, but they did at least escape the everlasting fire from the ground. Above all he sympathized with the swarms of human beings crawling and falling in the sea of mud below.

He took off and proceeded to the sector allotted to the squadron, and where four of its machines now lay in heaps of wreckage. For some minutes he flew up and down the Line, trying to pick out the new British advance posts, for the enemy were still retiring; it would be an easy matter to make a mistake and shoot up the hard-won positions that a few days before had been in German hands.

Archie and field-guns began to cough and bark as he approached the new German front Line, and machine-guns chattered shrilly, but he was past caring about such things. There was no way of avoiding them; they were just evils that had to be borne. One hoped for the best and carried on.

The battle was still raging. It was difficult to distinguish between the British and German troops, they seemed so hopelessly intermingled, so he turned farther into German territory rather than risk making a mistake.

He found a trench in which a swarm of troops were feverishly repairing the parapet, and forced them to seek cover. Then he turned sharp to the right and broke up another working-party; there were no more long convoys to attack, but he found a German staff car and chased it until the driver, taking a corner too fast in his efforts to escape, overturned it in a ditch.

For some minutes he worried a battery of field-guns that were taking up a new position. Then he turned back towards the Lines—or the stretch of No Man's Land that had originally marked the trench system.

He was still half a mile away when it happened. Just what it was he could not say, although Mark swore it was one of the new 'chain' archies—two phosphorus flares joined together by a length of wire that wrapped itself around whatever it struck, and set it on fire. The Bristol lurched sickeningly, and for a moment went out of control.

White-faced, Biggles fought with the control-stick to get the machine on even keel again, for at his height of a thousand feet there was very little margin of safety. He had just got the machine level when a wild yell and a blow on the back of his head brought him round, staring.

Aft of the gunner's cockpit the machine was a raging sheet of flame, which Mark was squirting with his Pyrene extinguisher, but without visible effect. As the extinguisher emptied itself of its contents he flung it overboard and set about beating the flames with his gauntlets.

Biggles did the only thing he could do in the circumstances; he jammed the control-stick forward and dived in a frantic effort to 'blow out' the flames with his slipstream. Fortunately his nose was still pointing towards the Lines, and the effort brought him fairly close, but the flames were only partly subdued and sprang to life again as he eased the control-stick back to prevent the machine from diving into the ground.

The Bristol answered to the controls so slowly that his wheels actually grazed the turf, and he knew at once what had happened. The flames had burnt through to his tail unit destroying the fabric on his elevators, rendering the fore and aft controls useless. He knew it was the end, and, abandoning hope of reaching the Lines, he concentrated his efforts on saving their lives. He thought and acted with a coolness that surprised him.

He tilted the machine on to its side, holding up his nose with the throttle, and commenced to slip wing-tip first towards the ground. Whether he was over British or German territory he neither knew nor cared; he had to get on to the ground or be burnt alive.

A quick glance behind revealed Mark still thrashing the flames with his glove, shielding his face with his left arm. Twenty feet from the ground Biggles switched off everything and unfastened his safety belt. The prop stopped. In the moment's silence he yelled 'Jump!'

He did not wait to see if Mark had followed his instructions, for there was no time, but climbed quickly out of his cockpit on to the wing just as the tip touched the ground. He had a fleeting vision of what seemed to be a gigantic catherine wheel as the machine cartwheeled over the ground, shedding struts and flaming canvas, and then he lay on his back, staring at the sky, gasping for breath.

For a ghastly moment he thought his back was broken, and he struggled to rise in an agony of suspense. He groaned as he fought for breath, really winded for the first time in his life.

Mark appeared by his side and clutched at his shoulders. 'What is it—what is it?' he cried, believing that his partner was mortally hurt.

Biggles could not speak, he could only gasp. Mark caught him by the collar and dragged him into a near-by trench. They fell in a heap at the bottom.

'Not hurt—winded!' choked Biggles. 'Where are we?'

Mark took a quick look over the parapet, and then jumped back, shaking his head. 'Dunno!' he said laconically. 'Can't see anybody. All in the trenches, I suppose.'

Biggles managed to stagger to his feet. 'We'd better lie low till we find out where we are!' he panted. 'What a mess! Let's get in here!' He nodded towards the gaping mouth of a dugout.

Footsteps were squelching through the mud towards them, and they dived into the dugout, Biggles leading. He knew instantly that the place was already occupied, but in the semi-darkness he could not for a moment make out who or what it was. Then he saw, and his eyes went round with astonishment. It was a German, cowering in a corner.

'*Kamerad! Kamerad!* cried the man, with his arms above his head.

'All right, we shan't hurt you,' Biggles assured him, kicking a rifle out of the way. 'It looks as if we're all in the same boat, but if you try any funny stuff I'll knock your block off!'

The German stared at him wide-eyed, but made no reply.

There was a great noise of splashing and shouting in the trench outside; a shell landed somewhere close at hand with a deafening roar, and a trickle of earth fell from the ceiling.

Mark grabbed Biggles' arm as a line of feet passed the entrance; there was no mistaking the regulation German boots, but if confirmation was needed, the harsh, guttural voices supplied it. They both breathed more freely as the feet disappeared and the noise receded.

123

'It looks as if we've landed in the middle of the war,' observed Biggles, with a watchful eye on the Boche, who still crouched in his corner as if dazed—as indeed he was.

'What are we going to do? We can't spend the rest of the war in here,' declared Mark.

'I wouldn't if I could,' replied Biggles. 'But it's no use doing anything in a hurry.'

'Some Boche troops will come barging in here in a minute and hand us a few inches of cold steel; they're not likely to be particular after that hullaballoo outside.'

Hullaballoo was a good word; it described things exactly. There came a medley of sounds in which shouts, groans, rifle and revolver shots and the reports of bursting hand-grenades could be distinguished.

'It sounds as if they're fighting all round us,' muttered Mark anxiously.

'As long as they stay round us I don't mind,' Biggles told him. 'It'll be when they start crowding in here that the fun will begin!'

Heavy footsteps continued to splash up and down the communication trench. Once a German officer stopped outside the dugout and Biggles held his breath. The Boche seemed to be about to enter, but changed his mind and went off at a run.

Then there came the sound of a sharp scuffle in the trench and a German N.C.O. leapt panting into the dugout. He glanced around wildly as the two airmen started up, and broke into a torrent of words. He was splashed with mud from head to foot, and bleeding from a cut in the cheek. He carried a rifle, but made no attempt to use it.

'Steady!' cried Biggles, removing the weapon from the man's unresisting hands. The Boche seemed to be trying to tell them something, pointing and gesticulating as he spoke.

'I think he means that his pals outside are coming in,' said Biggles with a flash of inspiration. "Well, there's still plenty of room.'

'Anybody in there?' cried a voice from the doorway.

Before Biggles could speak the German had let out a yell.

124

'Just share this among you, but don't quarrel over it!'
went on the same voice.

'This' was a Mills bomb that pitched on to the floor
between them.

There was a wild stampede for the door; Biggles slipped,
and was the last out. He had just flung himself clear as
the dugout went up with a roar that seemed to burst his
ear-drums. He looked up to see the point of a bayonet a
few inches from his throat; behind it was the amazed face
of a British Tommy.

The soldier let out a whistle of surprise. More troops
came bundling round the corner of the trench, an officer
among them. 'Hallo, what's all this?' he cried, halting in
surprise.

'Don't let us get in your way,' Biggles told him quickly.
'Go on with the war!'

'What might you be doing here?'

'We might be blackberrying, but we're not. Again, we
might be playing croquet, or roller-skating, but we're not.
We're just waiting.'

'Waiting! What for?'

'For you blokes to come along, of course. I've got a date
with a bath and a bar of soap, so I'll be getting along.'

'You'd better get out of this,' the other told him, grinning, as he prepared to move on.

'That's what I thought!' declared Biggles. 'Perhaps
you'd tell us the easiest and safest way?'

The other laughed. 'Sure I will,' he said. 'Keep straight
on down that sap we've just come up and you'll come to
our old Line. It's all fairly quiet now.'

'So I've noticed,' murmured Biggles. 'Come on, Mark,
let's get back to where we belong.'

'What about the Bristol?' asked Mark.

'What about it? Are you thinking of carrying it back
with you? I didn't stop to examine it closely, as you may
have noticed, but I fancy that kite, or what's left of it, will
take a bit of sticking together again. We needn't worry
about that. The repair section will collect it, if it's any good.
Come on!'

Three hours later, weary and smothered with mud, they

arrived back at the aerodrome, having got a lift part of the way on a lorry.

Mabs, on crutches, was standing at the door of the mess. 'Where have you been?' he asked.

'Ha! Where haven't we!' replied Biggles, without stopping.

'Where are you off to now in such a hurry?' called Mabs after him.

'To bed, laddie,' Biggles told him enthusiastically. 'To bed, till you find me another aeroplane.'

The Pup's First Flight

WHEN THE TIME CAME for Biggles to leave his old squadron and say good-bye to Mark Way, his gunner, he found himself a good deal more depressed than he had thought possible; he realized for the first time just how attached to them he had become. Naturally, he had been delighted to join a scout squadron, for he had always wanted to fly single-seaters. The presence of his old pal, Mahoney, who was flight-commander, prevented any awkwardness or strangeness amongst his new comrades, and he quickly settled down to routine work.

The commanding officer, Major Mullen, of his new squadron, No 266, stationed at Maranique, allowed none of his pilots to take unnecessary risks if he could prevent it. So he gave Biggles ten days in which to make himself proficient in the handling of the single-seater Pup that had been allocated to him.

Biggles was told to put in as much flying-time as possible, but on no account to cross the Lines, and he found that the enforced rest from eternal vigilance did him a power of good, for his nerves had been badly jarred by his late spell of trench strafing.

By the end of a week he was thoroughly at home with the Pup, and ready to try his hand at something more serious than beetling up and down behind his own Lines. He had noted all the outstanding landmarks around Maranique, and once or twice he accompanied Mahoney on practice formation flights. His flight-commander had expressed himself satisfied, and Biggles begged to be allowed to do a 'show.'

His chance came soon. Lorton was wounded in the arm

127

and packed off to hospital, and Biggles was detailed to take his place the following morning. But the afternoon before this decision took effect he had what he regarded as a slice of luck that greatly enhanced his reputation with the C.O., and the officers of the squadron, as well as bringing his name before Wing Headquarters.

He had set off on a cross-country flight to the Aircraft Repair Section at St. Omer, to make inquiries for the equipment officer about a machine that had gone back for reconditioning, when he spotted a line of white archie bursts at a very high altitude—about 15,000 feet, he judged it to be.

He was flying at about 5,000 a few miles inside the Lines at the time, and he knew that the archie was being fired by British guns, which could only mean that the target was an enemy aircraft. It seemed to be flying on a course parallel with the Lines, evidently on a photographic or scouting raid.

Without any real hope of overtaking it he set off in pursuit, and, knowing that sooner or later the German would have to turn to reach his own side he steered an oblique course that would bring him between the raider and the Lines. In a few minutes he had increased his height to 10,000 feet, and could distinctly see the enemy machine. It was a Rumpler two-seater. He had no doubt that the observer had spotted him, but the machine continued on its way as if the pilot was not concerned, possibly by reason of his superior altitude.

Biggles began to edge a little nearer to the Lines, and was not much more than a thousand feet below the Hun, when, to his disgust, it turned slowly and headed off on a diagonal course towards No Man's Land.

The Pup was climbing very slowly now, and it was more with hope than confidence that Biggles continued the pursuit. Then the unexpected happened. The enemy pilot turned sharply and dived straight at him, but opened fire at much too great a range for it to be effective, although he held the burst for at least a hundred rounds. Biggles had no idea where the bullets went, but he saw the Hun, at the end of his dive, zoom nearly back to his original altitude, and then make for home at full speed. But he had lingered just a trifle too long.

Biggles climbed up into the 'blind' spot under the enemy's elevators, and although the range was still too long for good shooting, he opened fire. Whether any of his shots took effect he was unable to tell, but the Hun was evidently alarmed, for the Rumpler made a quick turn out of the line of fire. It was a clumsy turn, and cost him two hundred precious feet of height at a moment when height was all-important. Moreover, it did not give the gunner in the back seat a chance to use his weapon.

Biggles seized his opportunity and fired one of the longest bursts he ever fired in his life. The German gunner swayed for a moment, then collapsed in his cockpit. Then, to his intense satisfaction, Biggles saw the propeller of the other machine slow down and stop, whereupon the enemy pilot shoved his nose down and dived for the Lines, now not more than two or three miles away.

It was a move that suited Biggles well, for the Rumpler was defenceless from the rear, so he tore down in hot pursuit, guns blazing, knowing that the Hun was at his mercy. The enemy pilot seemed to realize this for he turned broadside on and threw up his hands in surrender.

Biggles was amazed, for although he had heard of such things being done it was his first experience of it. He ceased firing at once and took up a position on the far side of the disabled machine; he did not trust his prisoner very much, for he guessed that he would, if the opportunity arose, make a dash for the Lines—so near, and yet so far away. Biggles therefore shepherded him down like a well-trained sheep-dog bringing in a stray lamb.

He could not really find it in his heart to blame the enemy pilot for surrendering. The fellow had had to choose between being made prisoner and certain death, and had chosen captivity as the lesser of the two evils. 'Death before capture,' is no doubt an admirable slogan, but it loses some of its attractiveness in the face of cold facts.

The German landed about four miles from Maranique and was prevented by a crowd of Tommies from purposely injuring his machine. Biggles landed in a near-by field and hurried to the scene, arriving just as the C.O. and several officers of the squadron, who had witnessed the end of the combat from the aerodrome, dashed up in the squadron car. It was purely a matter of luck that Major Raymond, of Wing Headquarters, who had been on the aerodrome talking with Major Mullen, was with them.

He smiled at Biggles approvingly. 'Good show!' he said. 'We've been trying to get hold of one of these machines intact for a long time.'

Biggles made a suitable reply and requested that the crew of the Rumpler should be well cared for. The pilot, whose name they learnt was Schmidt, looked morose and bad-tempered—as, indeed, he had every cause to be; the observer had been wounded in the chest and was unconscious.

They were taken away under escort in an ambulance, and that was the end of the affair. Biggles never learned what happened to them.

The offensive patrol for which he had been detailed in place of Lorton turned out to be a more difficult business. It began quite simply. He took his place in a formation of five machines, and for an hour or more they cruised up and down their sector without incident, except, of course, for the inevitable archie. Then the trouble started around a single machine.

Several times they had passed a British machine—an R.E.8—circling over the same spot, obviously engaged in doing a 'shoot' for the artillery, and Biggles was able to sympathize with the pilot. He watched the circling 'plane quite dispassionately for a moment or two, glanced away, and then turned back to the R.E.8. It was no longer there.

He stared—and stared harder. Then he saw it, three thousand feet below, plunging earthwards in flames. Screwing his head round a little farther he made out three German Albatros streaking for home. They must have made their attack on the two-seater under the very noses of the Pups, and, well satisfied with the result of their work, were removing themselves from the vicinity without loss of time. But they were well below the Pups, and Mahoney, who was leading, tore down after them in a screaming dive, closely followed by the rest of the formation.

As they went down, something—he could not say what—made Biggles, who was an outside flank man, look back over his shoulder. There was really no reason why he should but the fact that he did so provided another example of the uncanny instinct he was developing for detecting the presence of Huns.

The sight that met his gaze put all thought of the escaping Albatros clean out of his head. A German High Patrol of not fewer than twenty Triplanes were coming down like the proverbial ton of bricks.

Biggles' first idea was to warn Mahoney of the impending onslaught, but, try as he would, he could not overtake his leader. Yet he knew that if the Huns were allowed to come on in a solid formation on their tails, most of them would be wiped out before they knew what had hit them. He could think of only one thing to do, and he did it, although it did not occur to him that he was making something very much like a deliberate sacrifice of his own life. That he was not killed was due no doubt to the very unexpectedness of his move, which temporarily disorganized the Hun 'circus.' He swung the Pup round on its axis, cocked up his nose to face the oncoming Huns, and let drive at the whole formation.

The leader swerved just in time to avoid head-on collision. His wing tip missed Biggles' by inches. The lightning turn threw the others out of their place, and they, too, had to swerve wildly to avoid collision with their leader.

Biggles held his breath as the cloud of gaudy-coloured enemy machines roared past him, so close that he could see the faces of the pilots staring at him. Yet not a bullet touched his machine. Nor did he hit one of them—at least, as far as he could see.

The Huns pulled up, hesitating, to see if their leader was going on after the other Pups or staying to slay the impudent one. At that moment, Mahoney, missing one of his men, looked back. In that quick flash it must have seemed to him that Biggles was taking on the entire German Air

131

Force single-handed, and he hung his Pup on its prop as he headed back towards the mêlée.

He knew what Biggles himself at that time did not know; that the German formation was the formidable Richthofen 'circus', led by the famous Baron himself, his conspicuous all-red Fokker triplane even then pouring lead at the lone Pup.

Biggles could never afterwards describe the sensation of finding himself in the middle of Germany's most noted air fighters. He was, as he put it, completely flummoxed. He merely shot at every machine that swam across his sights, wondering all the while why his Pup did not fall to pieces.

The reason why it did not was probably that put forward by Captain Albert Ball, V.C., in defence of his method of plunging headlong into the middle of an enemy 'circus'. Such tactics temporarily disorganized the enemy formation, and the pilots dared not shoot as freely as they would normally for fear of hitting or colliding with their own men. Be that as it may, in the opening stage of the uproar Biggles' Pup was hit less than a dozen times, and in no place was it seriously damaged.

By the time the Huns sorted themselves out Mahoney and the other three Pups were on the scene. Even so, the gallant action of the leader in taking on such overwhelming odds would not have availed had it not been for the opportune arrival of a second formation of Pups and a squadron of Bristols—Biggles' old squadron, although he did not know it. That turned the tide.

The huge dog-fight lost height quickly, as such affairs nearly always did, and was soon down to five thousand feet. It was impossible for any pilot to know exactly what was happening; each man picked an opponent and stuck to him as long as he could. If he lost him he turned to find another.

That was precisely what Biggles did, and it was utterly out of the question for him to see if he shot anyone down. If a machine at which he was shooting fell out of the fight, someone else was shooting at him before he could determine whether his Hun was really hit or merely shamming.

He saw more than one machine spinning, and two or three smoke-trails where others had gone down in flames. He also saw a Bristol and a triplane that had collided whirling down together in a last ghastly embrace.

At four thousand feet he pulled out, slightly dizzy, and tried to make out what was happening. He picked out Mahoney by his streamers, not far away, and noted that the fight seemed to be breaking up by mutual consent. Odd machines were still circling round each other, but each leader was trying to rally his men.

Mahoney, in particular, was trying frantically to attract the attention of the surviving members of his patrol, for the fight had drifted over German territory and it was high time to see about getting nearer the Lines.

Biggles took up position on Mahoney's flank, and presently another Pup joined them. Of the other two there was no sign.

The Bristols were already streaming back towards home in open formation, and Mahoney followed them. They passed the charred remains of the R.E.8 that had been the cause of all the trouble, gaunt and black in the middle of No Man's Land. They reached the Lines and turned to fly parallel with them.

Their patrol was not yet finished, but all the machines had been more or less damaged, so after waiting a few minutes to give the other two Pups a chance of joining them if they were still in the air, they turned towards the aerodrome. It was as well they did, for Biggles' engine began to give trouble, although by nursing it he managed to reach home.

They discovered that the squadron had already been informed of the dog-fight, artillery observers along the Line reporting that five British and seven German machines had been seen to fall. There seemed little chance of the two missing Pups turning up. The surviving members of the patrol hung about the tarmac for some time, but they did not return. That evening they were reported 'missing.'

Caught Napping

'HOW OFTEN DO you run into shows as big as that?' Biggles asked Mahoney, at lunch.

'Oh, once in a while! Not every day, thank goodness!' replied Mahoney. 'Why?'

'I was just wondering.' Biggles ruminated a minute or two. 'You know, laddie, we do a lot of sneering at the Huns, and say they've no imagination.'

'What about it?'

'Well, I'm not so sure about it, that's all.'

'What! You turning pro-Hun, or something?'

'But it seems to me they're using their brains more than we are.'

'How?'

'We just fly and fight, and that's all we think about.'

'What do you mean?'

'Well, in the first place, the Huns mostly stay over their own side of the Lines, knowing that we'll go over to them. How often do you see a big formation of Hun scouts over this side? Mighty seldom. That isn't just luck. That's a clever policy laid down by the German higher authority.

'Then there's this grouping of their hot-stuff pilots into "circuses". And the way that bunch arrived this morning wasn't a fluke—you can bet your life on that. It was all very neatly arranged. Can't you see the idea? The old R.E.8 was the meat; three Huns go down after it just when they knew we were about due back, and that we were certain to follow them—go down after them. It pans out just as they expected, and off they go, taking us slap under the big mob who were sitting up topsides waiting for us. Although I say it as shouldn't, it was a bit of luck I happened to look back. As it turned out, the Hun plan went off at half-cock, but it might not have done. That's why I say these tripe-hound merchants are flying with their heads.'

'Well, I can't stop 'em, if that's what you mean.'

'I never suggested you could, did I? But there's nothing to prevent us exercising our grey matter a bit, is there?'

'You're right, kid,' joined in Maclaren, another flight-commander, who had overheard the conversation. 'You're absolutely dead right!'

'I think I am,' replied Biggles frankly. 'War-flying is too new for strategy to be laid down in the text-books; we've got to work it out for ourselves.'

'What's all this?' asked Major Mullen, who had entered the room and caught the last part of the conversation.

Briefly, Maclaren gave him the gist of the conversation. The C.O. nodded as he listened, then he looked at Biggles.

'What do you suggest?' he asked.

'Well, sir, it seems to me we might have a word with the other scout squadrons about it, and work out a scheme. At present we all do our shows independently, so to speak, but if we could work out a plot together—an ambush, if you like, like the Huns did this morning—we might give the tripe merchants over the way something to think about. If we did happen to catch them properly it would have the effect of making them chary about tackling odd machines for a bit. They'd always be worried for fear they were heading into a trap.'

'That sounds like common-sense to me,' agreed the C.O. 'All right, Bigglesworth, you work out the plot and submit it to me, and I'll see what can be done about it. But we shall have to keep it to ourselves. If Wing heard about it they'd probably knock it on the head, on the ground that such methods were irregular, although perhaps I shouldn't say that.'

'We all know it, sir, without you saying it, anyway!' grinned Biggles.

After dinner he sat down with a pencil and paper to work out his 'plot', and before he went to bed he had the scheme cut and dried. It was fairly simple, as he explained to the others in the morning, and based upon the methodical habits of the enemy, and the assumption that the other scout squadrons would co-operate.

'From my own personal observation,' he explained, 'the Huns—by which I mean the "circuses", particularly the Richthofen crowd which is stationed at Douai—do two big shows a day. Sometimes, when things are lively, they do three. They always do a big evening show, one that finishes about sunset, just before they pack up for the night. Very well. It gets dark now about half past six. That means that the Huns must leave the ground on their last show between four and four-thirty. Now, if they have a dog-fight they don't all go home together, but do the same as we do— trickle home independently, in twos and threes. They did that this morning. I saw them. Now, I reckon that the last place they'd expect big trouble would be on the way home, near their own aerodrome, and that's where I propose to spring the surprise packet.

'To carry out my idea with maximum safety, it would need three squadrons—four would be even better. This is the way of it: At four o'clock one squadron pushes along to some pre-arranged sector of the Line, and makes itself a nuisance—shooting up the Hun trenches, or something to make itself conspicuous. The Hun artillery observers will see this, of course, and are almost certain to ring up the Richthofen headquarters to say there is a lot of aerial activity on their bit of Front. It stands to reason that the circus will at once make for that spot; give them their due they don't shirk a rough-house. Right-ho. The squadron that is kicking up the fuss keeps its eyes peeled for the Huns. It'll pretend not to see them until they're fairly close. Then they scatter, making towards home. The Huns are almost bound to split up to chase them, and our fellows can please themselves whether or not they stay and fight. But they must remember that their job is to split up the Huns.

'As soon as this business is well under way, the other two—or three—squadrons will take off, climb to the limit of their height, and head over the Lines on a course that'll bring them round by Douai. Get the idea? The Huns will think the show's over and come drifting home in small parties, without keeping very careful watch. We shall be there to meet them. Huns on the ground may see us, but they won't be able to warn the fellows in the air. In that way, if the scheme works out as I've planned it, we shall catch these pretty birds bending when they're least expecting it. That's all. If the worst comes to the worst we should be no worse off than we are on an ordinary show, when we always seem to be outnumbered. At the best, we shall give the Huns a shock they'll remember for some time. What do you think about it, sir?'

'I certainly think there is a good deal to be said for it,' agreed the major. 'I'll speak to the other squadrons. Perhaps your old squadron would oblige by kicking up the fuss with their Bristols. then, if 287, with their S.E.s, and 231, and ourselves, get behind the Huns we shall at least be sure of meeting them on even terms, even if they do happen to keep in one formation. All right; leave it to me. I'll see what I can do.'

It took nearly a week of conferences to bring the scheme to a stage where it was ready to be tried out, but at last, burning with impatience and excitement, Biggles made his way to the sheds with the others for the big show.

Watches had been carefully synchronized on the instrument boards of all pilots taking part, and every possible precaution taken to prevent a miscarriage of plans. Major Paynter, of Biggles' old squadron, had agreed to send every Bristol he could raise into the air, to make itself as obnoxious as possible at a given spot, at the arranged time.

The others were to rendezvous over Maranique in 'layer' formation (machines flying in tiers) at four-thirty—No. 266 Squadron at ten thousand feet, 231 Squadron at thirteen thousand feet, and 287 Squadron at sixteen thousand feet. Major Mullen was leading the whole show on a roundabout course that would bring them behind the enemy, assuming, of course, that the enemy circus would concentrate in the area where the Bristols were to lure them.

Three-quarters of an hour later, Major Mullen swung round in a wide circle that brought them actually within sight of Douai, the headquarters of the most famous fighting scouts in the German Imperial Air Service. Biggles never forgot the scene. The sun was low in the west, sinking in a crimson glow. A slight mist was rising, softening the hard outlines of roads, woods, hedges, and fields below, as though seen through a piece of lilac-tinted gauze. To the east, the earth was already bathed in deep purple and indigo shadows.

No enemy aircraft were in sight, not even on the ground, as they turned slowly over the peaceful scene to seek the enemy in the glowing mists of the west. They had not long to wait.

Biggles saw two Triplanes, flying close together, slowly materialize in the mist, like goldfish swimming in a pale milky liquid. The enemy pilots were gliding down, probably with their eyes on the aerodrome, and it is doubtful if they even saw the full force of British machines that had assembled to overwhelm them. Biggles felt almost sorry for them as Major Mullen shook his wings, as a signal, and the nine Pups roared down on the unsuspecting Triplanes.

It was impossible to say which machine actually scored most hits. One Triplane broke up instantly. The other jerked upwards as if the pilot had been mortally wounded, turned slowly over on to its back, plunged downwards in a vicious spin with its engine full on and bored into the ground two miles below.

The Pups resumed formation and returned to their original height and course. Another Triplane emerged from the mist, but something evidently caught the pilot's eye—perhaps the sun flashing on a wing—and he looked upwards. He acted with the speed of light and flung his machine into a spin to seek safety on the ground. The Pups did not follow, for the Triplane was far below them and they would not risk getting too low so far over the Line.

A few minutes later a straggling party of seven machines appeared, followed at a distance by five more. It was obvious from the loose formation in which they were flying that they considered themselves quite secure so near their nest. They, too, must have been looking at the ground, and Biggles was amazed at the casual manner in which they

138

continued flying straight on with death literally raining on them from the sky.

He picked out his man and poured in a long burst of bullets before the pilot had time to realize his peril. A cloud of smoke quickly followed by flame, burst from the Triplane's engine. Biggles zoomed upwards and looked back. The seven machines had disappeared. Two long pillars of smoke marked the going of at least two of them.

How many had actually fallen he was unable to tell. Away to the left the other five Triplanes were milling around in a circle, hotly pursued by the second squadron of Pups, whilst the S.E.s were sitting slightly above, waiting to pounce on any enemy machine that tried to leave the combat.

It was the last real surprise of the day, not counting a lonely straggler that they picked up near the Lines and which they had sent down under a tornado of lead. Biggles quite definitely felt sorry for that pilot. Two or three more machines had appeared while the main combat was in progress, but the dog-fight had lost height, and they saw it at once, so were able to escape by spinning down.

The engagement really resolved itself into the sort of show that Biggles had anticipated. The enemy had been caught napping, and many of them had paid the penalty. The three squadrons of British machines reached the Line at dusk, without a single casualty and almost unscathed. One machine only, an S.E.5 of 287 Squadron, had to break formation near the Lines with a piece of archie shrapnel in its engine. Except for that, the Pups and S.E.s returned home in a formation as perfect as when they started.

Congratulations flew fast and furious when Major Mullen's squadron landed, for it had unquestionably been one of the most successful 'shows' ever undertaken by the squadron. A quick comparison of notes revealed that seven Triplanes had been destroyed for certain, either having been seen to crash or fall in flames. How many others had been damaged, or enemy pilots wounded, they had, of course, no means of knowing.

But the most successful part of the issue was that not a single British machine had been lost. Major Mullen thanked Biggles personally and congratulated him on his initiative, in the Squadron Office, in front of the other pilots.

'Well, I'm glad it has turned out as I hoped it would, sir. We've given the Huns something to talk about in mess to-night. Maybe they won't be quite so chirpy in future!' observed Biggles modestly.

The party was about to break up when Watt Tyler, the Recording Officer, hurried into the room waving a strip of paper above his head; his eyes were shining as he laid it on the C.O.'s desk.

Major Mullen read the signal, and a grim smile spread over his face. 'Gentlemen,' he said, 'I am glad to be able to tell you that we shall be able to give the Huns something else to think about before long; the squadron is to be equipped with the long-secret super-scout at last. Our Pups are to be replaced by Sopwith Camels.'

A moment's silence greeted this important announcement.

It was broken by Biggles. 'Fine!' he said. 'Now we'll show the Huns what's what!'

The Yellow Hun

No. 266 SQUADRON, R.F.C., at Maranique, had been equipped with Sopwith Camels for nearly a month, and with the improved equipment the pilots were showing the enemy—as Biggles had put it—what was what. Except for two pilots who had been killed whilst learning to fly the very tricky Camels, things had gone along quite smoothly, and Biggles had long ago settled down as a regular member of the squadron. Indeed, he was beginning to regard himself as something of a veteran.

It was a warm spring afternoon, and as he sat sunning himself on the veranda after an uneventful morning patrol he felt on good terms with himself and the world in general. 'Where's the Old Man?' he suddenly asked Mahoney, who had just returned from the sheds, where he had been supervising the timing of his guns.

'Dunno,' was the reply. 'I think he's gone off to Amiens, or somewhere, for a conference. Oh, here he comes now. He looks pretty grim. I'll bet something's in the wind!'

The C.O. joined them on the veranda. He looked at Biggles as if he were about to speak, but he changed his mind and looked through the open window into the anteroom, where several other officers were sitting. He called to them to come outside.

'I've a bit of news—or perhaps I should say a story,' he began, when everyone had assembled. 'It will be of particular interest to you, Bigglesworth.'

Biggles stared. 'To me, sir?' he cried in surprise.

'Yes. You haven't been over to your old squadron lately, have you?'

Biggles shook his head. 'No, sir, I haven't!' he said wonderingly.

'Then you haven't heard about Way?'

'Mark Way!' Biggles felt his face going white. Mark had been his gunner and great friend when they were together in 169 Squadron. 'Why, he isn't——?' He could not bring himself to say the fatal word.

'No, he isn't dead, but he'll never fly again,' said the C.O. quietly.

Biggles' lips turned dry. 'But how—what?' he stammered.

'I've just seen him,' went on the C.O. 'I had to attend a conference in Amiens, and I ran into Major Paynter, who was going to the hospital to see Way. He told me about it. Way is now en route for England. He'll never come back.'

'But I don't understand!' exclaimed Biggles. 'He was due to go home when I came here; he was going to get his pilot's wings. In fact I thought he'd actually gone.'

'That's right,' said the C.O. 'He packed up his kit and set off, but apparently he was kept hanging about the port of embarkation for some time. Then the Huns made their big show, and he with everyone else who was waiting to go home was recalled to the squadron.'

'But why didn't he let me know?' cried Biggles.

'He hadn't time. He arrived back just in time to be sent on a show with Captain Mapleton. They didn't return, and were posted missing the same day. Way arrived back yesterday, having crawled into our front line trench, minus his right hand and an eye.'

'Good heavens!'

'He asked to be remembered to you, and said he would write to you as soon as he was able, from home.'

'But what happened, sir?'

'I'm coming to that. In point of fact, what I'm about to say was intended for you alone—his last message—but I think it is a matter that concerns everyone, so I shall make no secret of it.' The C.O.'s face hardened. 'This is what he told me,' he continued. 'As I said, he was flying with Mapleton——'

142

'Where's Mapleton now?' broke in Biggles.

'Mapleton was killed. But let me continue.'

Biggles gripped the rail of the veranda, but said nothing.

'He was, I say, acting as gunner for Mapleton,' went on the C.O. 'They were attacked by a big bunch of enemy machines, near Lille. By a bit of bad luck they got their engine shot up in the early stages of the fight, and had to go down, and the Hun who had hit them followed them down, shooting at them all the time. Their prop had stopped, and they waved to him to show that they were going to land, but he continued shooting at them while they were, so to speak, helpless.'

A stir ran through the listeners.

'It was at this juncture that Way was struck in the eye by a piece of glass; but he didn't lose consciousness. Mapleton made a perfect landing in spite of the damage the machine had suffered and it looked as if they would both escape with their lives—as indeed they would have done. But the Hun thought differently. Thank Heaven they are not all like him. He deliberately shot them up after they had landed—emptied his guns at them.'

'The unspeakable hog!' Biggles ground the words out through clenched teeth.

'Mapleton fell dead with a bullet through the head. Way's wrist was splintered by an explosive bullet, and his hand was subsequently amputated in a German field hospital. Three days ago, on the eve of being transferred to a prison camp, he escaped, and managed to work his way through the Lines. He arrived in a state of collapse, and Major Paynter thinks that it was only the burning desire to report the flagrant breach of the accepted rules of air fighting, and the passion for revenge, which he knew would follow, that kept him on his feet. The Hun seems to have been a Hun in every sense of the word; he actually went and gloated over Way in hospital.'

'Mark didn't learn his name, by any chance?' muttered Biggles harshly.

'Yes. It's Von Kraudil, of Jagdstaffel Seventeen.'

'What colour was his kite?' asked Biggles, his hands twitching curiously.

143

'Yes, that's more important, for by this we shall be able to recognize him.' The C.O. spoke softly, but very distinctly. 'He flies a sulphur-yellow Albatros with a black nose, and a black diamond painted on each side of the fuselage.'

'I've seen that skunk!' snarled McLaren, starting up. 'Yellow is a good colour for him. I'll——'

The C.O. held up his hands as a babble of voices broke out. 'Yes, I know,' he said quickly. 'Most of us have seen this machine; it's been working on this part of the Front for some time, so I hope it is still about.'

'I'll nail his yellow hide up in the ante-room!' declared Mahoney.

'Such methods would have been in order a few hundred years ago, but we can hardly do that sort of thing to-day,' smiled the C.O. 'All the same, a piece of yellow fuselage might look well——'

'Leave that to me, sir!' interrupted Biggles. 'Mark Way was my——'

'Not likely! No fear!' A chorus of protests from the other pilots overwhelmed him, and the C.O. was again compelled to call for silence. 'It's up to everyone to get him,' he went on. 'And the officer who gets him may have a week's leave!'

'I'll get that leave—to go and see Mark!' declared Biggles.

'All right, gentlemen, that's all,' concluded the C.O.

'He says that's all!' muttered Biggles to Mahoney. 'It isn't, not by a long shot!'

Under the influence of his cold fury his first idea was to rush off into the air and stay there until he had found the yellow Hun. Instead, he controlled himself, and made his way to his room to think the matter over. He was in a curious state of nerves, for the news had stirred him as nothing had ever done before. He was depressed by the tragic end of the man whom he still regarded as his best friend, and with whom he had had so many thrilling adventures. And tears actually came into his eyes when he thought of his old flight-commander, Mapleton, whom they all called Mabs, one of the most brilliant and fearless air fighters in France.

He was suffering from a mild form of shock, although he did not know it, and behind it all was the burning desire for vengeance. That by his cold-blooded action the yellow Hun had signed his own death warrant Biggles did not doubt, for not a single member of either his old squadron or his present one would rest until Mabs had been avenged. But Biggles wanted to shoot the man down himself. He wanted to see the tracer bullets boring into that yellow cockpit. The mere fact that the Hun had fallen under the guns of someone else would not give him the same satisfaction. In fact, as he pondered the matter, he began to feel afraid that someone else might shoot the Hun down before he could come to grips with him.

The matter was chiefly his concern, after all, he reasoned. Mark had been his friend, and Mabs his flight-commander. No doubt machines were already scouring the sky for the murderer—for that was almost what the action of shooting at a machine on the ground amounted to.

'Well,' he muttered at last, 'if I'm going to get this hound I'd better see about it!'

He rose, washed, picked up his flying kit, and made his way to the sheds. 'Where's everybody?' he asked Smyth, the flight-sergeant.

'In the air, sir.'

'Ah, I might have known it,' breathed Biggles. He was so accustomed to the sound of aero engines that he had hardly noticed the others taking off. But he knew only too well why the aerodrome was deserted, and he hastened to his own machine.

Within five minutes he was in his Camel, heading for the Line. He hardly expected to find Von Kraudil cruising about the sky alone; that would be asking too much. He would certainly be flying with a formation of single-seaters. If that were so, he, Biggles, would stand a better chance of finding his man by flying alone, as the Huns would certainly attack the lone British machine if they saw him, whereas they might refuse to engage the others if they were flying together.

145

In any case, a wide area would have to be combed, for the enemy machines operated far to the east and west of their base. So in order to expedite matters, Biggles deliberately asked for trouble by thrusting deep into the enemy country. Ground observers could hardly fail to see him, and would, he hoped, report his presence to the nearest squadrons, in accordance with their usual practice.

Far and wide he searched, but curiously enough the sky appeared to be deserted. Once he saw a formation of three Camels, and a little later three more, but he did not join them. Never had he seen the sky so empty.

At the end of two hours he was forced to return to the aerodrome without having seen an enemy aircraft of any sort, and consequently without firing a shot. On the ground he learned that the other machines had already returned, refuelled, and taken off again.

Then he had a stroke of luck—or so he regarded it. His tanks had been filled, and he was about to take off again, when Watt Tyler rushed out of the Squadron Office and hailed him. 'You're looking for that yellow devil, I suppose?' he inquired shortly.

'Who else do you suppose I'd be looking for?' replied Biggles coldly.

'All right, keep your hair on! I was only going to tell you that forward gunner observers have just reported that a large enemy formation has just crossed our Lines in pursuit of two Camels.'

'Where?'

'Up by Passchendaele.'

Biggles did not stop to thank Watt for the information. He thrust the throttle open, and as his wheels left the ground he soared upwards in a steep climbing turn in the direction of the well-known town.

He saw the dog-fight afar off. At least, he saw the archie bursts that clustered thickly about the isolated machines, and he roared towards the spot on full throttle, peering ahead round his windscreen to try to identify the combatants. Presently he was able to make out what had happened, for the two Camels that had been pursued had turned, and were now hard at it, assisted by half a dozen

146

Bristols. There seemed to be about twelve or fourteen Huns, all Albatroses. He guessed that they had chased the Camels over the Line, and, on turning, found their retreat cut off by the Bristols. That, in fact, was exactly what had happened.

The enemy machines were still too far away for their colours to be distinguished, but as he drew nearer he saw one, dark blue in colour, break out of the fight some distance below him and streak for the Line.

'Not so fast!' growled Biggles, as he altered his course slightly and tore down after the escaping Hun. The enemy pilot, who did not even see him, was leaning out of his cockpit on the opposite side of the fuselage, looking back at the dog-fight as if he expected the other machines to follow, and wondered why they did not. For a few seconds he omitted to watch the sky around him and paid the penalty for that neglect—as so many pilots did, sooner or later.

Biggles fired exactly five rounds at point-blank range, and the Hun's petrol tank burst into flames. Biggles zoomed clear, amazed at the effectiveness of his fire, for hitherto he had fired many rounds before such a thing had happened. His first shot must have gone straight through the tank. He glanced down, to see the Hun still falling, the doomed pilot leaning back in his cockpit with his arms over his face. It crashed in a sheet of flame near a British rest camp, and Biggles turned again to the dog-fight, which had now become more scattered over a fairly wide area.

Several Huns had broken out of the fight and were racing towards the Lines. But, as far as Biggles could see, there was not a yellow one amongst them, although he wasted some precious time chasing first one and then another in the hope of recognizing the particular one he sought. He turned back towards the spot where several machines were still circling, and as he drew nearer he saw something that would normally have given him the greatest satisfaction, but on this occasion brought a quick frown on his forehead. With a quick movement of his left hand he pushed up his goggles to make quite certain that he was not mistaken. But there was no mistake about it.

A bright yellow Hun had broken clear of the fight, but was being furiously attacked by a Camel—which Biggles instantly recognized by its markings as the one belonging to Mahoney. He had never seen a Camel handled like it before, and he sensed the hatred that possessed its pilot and inspired such brilliant flying.

The Hun hadn't a ghost of a chance; it was outmanœuvred at every turn. Once, as if to make suspicion a certainty, it turned broadside on towards Biggles, who saw a large black diamond painted on its yellow wooden side. That the Hun would fall was certain. It was only a matter of time, for the Camel was glued to its tail, guns spouting tracer bullets in long, vicious bursts. The pilot of the yellow machine seemed to be making no effort to retaliate but concentrated his efforts in attempting to escape, twisting and turning like a fish with an otter behind it.

Biggles had no excuse for butting-in, and he knew it. Mahoney was quite capable of handling the affair himself, and his presence might do more harm than good. If he got in the way of the whirling machines, the two Camel pilots would certainly have to watch each other to avoid collision, and in the confusion the Hun might escape.

That was a contingency Biggles dared not risk, much as he would have liked to take a hand. So he kept clear, and, circling, watched the end of a very one-sided duel. Suddenly, in a last frantic effort to escape, the Hun spun, came out, and spun again; but the Camel had spun down behind it and was ready to administer the knock-out. Mahoney let drive again, but the Hun did not wait for any more. Once again he spun, only to pull out at the last minute, then drop in a steep sideslip to a rather bad landing in a handy field.

Biggles, who had followed the fight down, beat the side of his cockpit with his clenched fist in impotent rage. 'The yellow skunk!' he grated. 'He's got away with it. Never mind, this is where Mahoney treats him to a spot of his own medicine.'

But Mahoney did nothing of the sort, as Biggles, in his heart, knew he would not. The flight-comander simply could not bring himself to shoot at a man who was virtually unarmed.

The knowledge that he, Biggles, could not either, made him still more angry, and with hate smouldering in his eyes, he dropped down and landed near Mahoney who had already put his machine on the ground not far from the Hun.

As they jumped from the cockpits and raced towards the yellow machine Biggles was afraid that Von Kraudil would set fire to his Albatros before they could reach him; but the Boche had no such intention, either because he forgot to do so, or because he was too scared.

'I got him!' roared Mahoney, as they ran.

'All right, I know you did. I'm not arguing about it, am I?' answered Biggles shortly. The fact that his flight-commander had shot down the yellow machine, the pilot of which, had after all escaped just retribution, was rather a bitter pill for him to swallow. He slowed down while still some yards away, for the German pilot certainly did not look the sort of man Biggles imagined he would be. He had taken off his cap and goggles and was leaning against the fuselage of his machine, face deadly pale. He was good-looking, flaxen-haired and blue-eyed—eyes now wide open with apprehension. A trickle of blood was running down his ashen cheek, and he endeavoured to stem it with a handkerchief while he looked from the two pilots to a crowd of Tommies who, with an officer at their head, were coming at the double across the field.

Mahoney eyed his prisoner coldly, but said nothing.

'What's your name?' snapped Biggles, eyes bright with hostility.

The German shook his head, making it clear that he did not understand.

Biggles pointed at the man. 'Von Kraudil?' he asked.

'Nein, nein!' was the reply.

Biggles looked at Mahoney, and Mahoney looked at Biggles.

'I don't believe it's him, after all!' declared Biggles. 'This kid doesn't look like a murderer to me. I say,' he

149

went on to the infantry officer, who now joined them, 'do you, or any of your fellows, happen to speak German?'

'I know a bit,' admitted the youthful, mud-splashed sub-altern.

'Then would you mind asking him his name?' requested Biggles.

The officer put the question to the Boche, and turned back to Biggles.

'He says he name is Schultz.'

'Ask him for his identification disc; I have special reasons for not wanting to make any mistake about this.'

Again the infantry officer addressed the German, who groped under his tunic and produced a small, round piece of metal.

'He's telling the truth,' went on the subaltern, after a quick glance at it. 'Here's his name right enough—Wilhelm Schultz.'

'Then ask him if he's flying Von Kraudil's machine.'

'No!' came the prompt reply from the subaltern, who had continued the interrogation. 'He says this used to be Von Kraudil's machine, but it was handed over to him the other day; Von Kraudil has a new one—a blue one.'

Biggles stared.

'Blue, did you say?'

The Hun stared from one to the other as the question was put to him, evidently unable to make out what the questions were leading up to.

'Yes. He says Von Kraudil's machine is blue, with a white diagonal bar behind the cross on the fuselage.'

'So that was Von Kraudil, eh?' mused Biggles softly.

'Why do you say "was"?' asked Mahoney.

'Because I got him after all!' cried Biggles exultantly. 'I got a machine answering to that description ten minutes ago! Come on, let's go and confirm it!'

'How did you manage to get mixed up in this affair?' asked Mahoney, as Biggles led the way to where the blue machine had crashed in flames. 'You were missing when the rest of us took off—asleep in your room, or something.'

'Asleep, my foot!' snorted Biggles. 'I was doing a spot of thinking—wondering what was the best way to get at that yellow Hun. It was sheer luck I heard about your dog-fight. I was making for my machine when Watt Tyler gave me the news that a formation of Huns was chasing two Camels. He gave me the direction so I beetled along. I saw the blue machine break away from the fight as I came up, went after it, and sent it down a flamer.'

'How about the pilot?' asked Mahoney. 'Did he manage to jump clear of his machine? If he didn't, we're going to have a job proving that Von Kraudil was flying it. We've only that other pilot's word for it that it was Von Kraudil's machine, you know.'

'H'm!' grunted Biggles. 'I hadn't thought of that. I certainly didn't see him jump, but he may have been flung clear when his machine crashed. Anyway,' he added, as the still smoking remains of the blue machine came into view, 'we'll soon know.'

A crowd of officers and men from the near-by rest camp were clustered around the remains. Forcing their way through the crowd, Mahoney and Biggles approached as near as they could to the hot debris of the machine. It was a terrible jumble of fused and twisted wires, utterly unrecognizable as an aeroplane.

'Gosh! What a mess!' muttered Biggles.

It was impossible to search the hot debris for the body of the pilot, and from the distance it was impossible to distinguish any sign of human remains. Mahoney turned to one of the officers. 'Can you tell me what happened to the pilot of this machine?' he asked.

'Why, yes,' replied the other. 'We found his body lying some distance away. He must have been killed when he was thrown out, but he had been badly burned beforehand. We took the body to the camp.'

'We want to find out his name,' said Mahoney. 'So we'll go along to the camp.'

'No need to do that,' said the officer. 'His name was Von Kraudil. I examined his identity disc.'

'Then it was our man, after all!' exclaimed Biggles. 'Come on; let's get back and report. I think I'll take that week's leave the Old Man spoke about—and go and see Mark.'

151

The Dawn Patrol

BIGGLES OPENED HIS EYES drowsily the next morning as a hand shook his shoulder respectfully but firmly. At the back of his sleep-soaked mind he knew it was his batman calling him.

'Come on, sir!' said a voice. 'It's six o'clock! Patrol leaves at half past!'

Biggles stared at the man coldly. 'Push off!' he said, and nestled lower under the bed-clothes.

'Come on, now, sir, drink your tea!' The batman held out the cup invitingly.

Biggles swung his legs over the side of the bed, shivering as the cold air struck his warm limbs, and took the tea. 'What's the weather like?' he asked.

'Not too good, sir; lot of cloud about, but no rain as yet!' Satisfied that his officer was really awake, the batman departed.

Biggles stood up and pulled on his sweater.

He hurried to the sheds and as he started up Mahoney appeared at the corner of a hangar.

'Trouble?' asked Biggles, noting the grim expression on Mahoney's face.

'Bunch of Huns are causing it,' replied Mahoney. 'Our job is to catch 'em and make 'em sorry. Come on.'

Mahoney climbed into his machine, looked around to see that the others were in place, taxied out on to the aerodrome, and roared into the air. The three other machines that were to form the dawn patrol took off behind him, heading towards the distant trenches of the western battle-front.

The grey light of early morning grew stronger, and before

the Lines were reached the sun was shining brightly. A strong wind was blowing from the west, bringing with it masses of cloud like great white cauliflowers, gleaming with gold and yellow at the top, merging into dark blue and purple at the base. Here and there the ground was still obscured by long grey blankets of ground mist, through which the earth showed in pale greens and browns.

The patrol climbed for some time before approaching the Lines, the leader making his way towards one of the strips of blue sky that here and there showed through the mass of cumulus. They entered the opening at five thousand feet, and then corkscrewed upwards, climbing steeply as though through a hollow tube to the top side of the cloud. Then the four machines levelled out and headed eastward.

Biggles, looking over the side, could see mile after mile of rolling white clouds, like great masses of cotton-wool, stretching away to the infinite distance where they cut a hard line against the blue sky. Below them, their four grey shadows, each surrounded by a complete rainbow, raced at incredible speed over the top of the gleaming vapour.

As far as he could see there were no other machines in the sky, although he was not quite certain that they had actually crossed the Lines yet. But Mahoney seemed to be flying on a steady course, and Biggles could not help admiring the confident manner in which his leader flew. He seemed to know exactly where he was, and what he was doing.

For some time they flew on, climbing gently, rounding mighty fantastic pyramids of cloud that seemed to reach to high heaven. Compared with them the 'planes were so small as to be negligible, like gnats flying round the base of snow-covered mountains, Biggles thought.

For twenty minutes or so Mahoney headed straight into German territory, turning neither to right nor left. The distance they had covered, with the wind behind them, could not be less than twenty miles; it would take them a long time to return with the wind in their teeth. Biggles wished there were some gaps in the clouds so that he might see the Lines, if they were in sight. They formed a barrier between the known and the unknown. On one side lay home, friends, and safety; on the other, mystery, enemies, and death.

From time to time, round, whirling balls of black smoke stained the cloudscape. They increased in size, becoming less dense as they did so, and then drifted into long plumes before they were finally dispersed by the wind. Archie. Biggles eyed it moodily, for although he no longer feared it, he never failed to regard it with suspicion. He fired a short burst downwards from his guns to warm them up and make sure they were in working order. From time to time the others did the same.

He was glad when at last Mahoney changed direction and began to fly north-west on a course nearly parallel with the Lines, a course that Biggles estimated would bring them back to the Lines some thirty miles above where they had crossed. The clouds seemed to increase in size in their new direction until they assumed colossal proportions. The patrol was now flying at nine thousand feet, but the summits of the clouds seemed to tower as far above them as the bases were below. Biggles had no idea that clouds could be so enormous.

They had been in the air for more than an hour, and so far they had not seen a single other machine, either friend or foe. Several times he squinted at the blinding sun between his first finger and thumb. This is too tame to be true, he thought, as he wiped the frozen breath from his wind-screen with the back of his glove, and worked his lips, which felt as if they were getting frost-bitten in the icy wind. He noticed that Mahoney was leading them to the very top of a stupendous pile of cloud that lay directly in their path.

He's going over it rather than round it—got an idea there's something on the other side, I suppose, thought Biggles, watching both sides of the gleaming mass. Yes, this is where we strike the rough stuff! he told himself. He did not know why he thought that. On the face of it there was no more reason to suppose that this particular cloud would conceal enemy aircraft any more than the others they had already passed. It may have been the instinct which he was beginning to develop that warned him. At any rate, something inside him seemed to say that hostile machines were not far away.

Mahoney was immediately over the top of the cloud-pile now, and Biggles could see him looking down at something below. Then he no longer thought of the cold, for Mahoney's machine was wobbling its wings. A red Very light soared into the air, the signal that enemy aircraft had been sighted.

Mahoney was banking now, turning slowly, and the other three machines swam into the spot where the leader had been a few moments before.

Biggles looked over the side, and caught his breath sharply as he found himself gazing into a hole in the clouds, a vast cavity that would have been impossible to imagine. It reminded him vaguely of the crater of a volcano of incredible proportions. Straight down for a sheer eight thousand feet the walls of opaque mist dropped, turning from yellow to brown, brown to mauve, and mauve to indigo at the basin-like depression in the remote bottom. The precipitous sides looked so solid that it seemed as if a man might try to climb down them, or rest on one of the shelves that jutted out at intervals.

He was so taken up with this phenomenon that for a brief space of time all else was forgotten. Then a tiny movement far, far below caught his eye, and he knew he was looking at that which the eagle-sighted flight-commander had seen instantly.

A number of machines—how many he could not tell—were circling round and round at the very bottom of the yawning crater, looking like microscopic fish at the bottom of a deep pool in a river. Occasionally one or more of them would completely disappear in the shadows, to reappear a moment later, wings flashing faintly as the light caught them. They were much too far away to distinguish whether they were friends or foes but Mahoney seemed to have no doubt in the matter. A tiny living spark of orange fire, flashing diagonally across the void, told its own story. It was a machine going down in flames, and that could only

155

mean one thing—a dog-fight was in progress in that well of mystery.

Then Mahoney went down, closely followed by the others.

Biggles never forgot that dive. There was something awe-inspiring about it. It was like sinking down into the very centre of the earth. There was insufficient room for the four machines to keep in a straight dive, as the cavity was not more than a few hundred yards across, so they were compelled to take a spiral course.

Down—down—down they went. Biggles thought they would never come to the end. The wind howled and screamed through struts and wires but he heeded it not. He was too engrossed in watching the tragedy being enacted below. Twice as they went down in that tremendous dive he saw machines fall out of the fight, leaving streamers of black smoke behind them, around which the others continued to turn and roll and shoot. There were at least twenty of them: drab biplanes with yellow wings, and rainbow-hued triplanes—red, green, blue, mauve, and even a white one.

Soon the dawn patrol was amongst the whirling machines, and it was every man for himself. Biggles picked out a group of Triplanes with black-crossed wings that were flying close together. They saw him coming and scattered like a school of minnows when a pike appears. He rushed at one of them, a blue machine with white wingtips, and pursued it relentlessly. His guns started chattering, and he saw the tracer bullets pouring straight into the centre of the fuselage of the machine below him. The Hun did not burst into flames, as he hoped it would. Instead, it zoomed upwards, turned slowly over on its back, and then, with the engine still on, spun down out of sight into the misty floor of the basin.

Biggles jerked up sharply and swerved just in time to avoid collision with a whirling bonfire of struts and canvas. His nostrils twitched as he hurtled through its smoking trail. He was shooting again, this time at the white machine. But the pilot was not to be so easily disposed of. He twisted and turned like a fish with a sea-lion after it, and more than once succeeded in getting in a burst of fire at him.

This was the hottest dog-fight in which Biggles had as yet taken part. The thought uppermost in his mind was he must inevitably collide with somebody in a moment. Already he had missed machines—Triplanes, F.E.s, and Pups—by inches. But the thought of a collision did not frighten him. He felt only a strange elation, a burning desire to go on doing this indefinitely—to down the enemy machines before he himself was killed, as he never doubted that he would be in the end. There was no thought in his mind of retreat or escape.

Something struck the machine with a force that made it quiver. The compass flew to pieces, and the liquid that it contained spurted back, half-blinding him. Mechanically he wiped his face with the back of his glove.

Where was the white Hun? He looked around, and his blood seemed to turn to ice at the sight that met his gaze. An F.E., a blazing meteor, was roaring nose-down across his front at a frightful speed. A black figure emerged from the flames with an arm flung over its face, and leapt outwards and downwards. The machine, almost as if it was still under control, deliberately swerved towards the white Triplane that was whirling across its front.

The Hun pilot saw his danger and twisted like lightning to escape. But he was too late. The blazing F.E. caught it fair and square across the fuselage. There was a shower of sparks and debris and a blinding flash of flame as the Triplane's tanks exploded. Then the two machines disappeared from Biggles' field of view.

For a moment he was stunned with shock, unable to think. With a mighty effort he pulled himself together, but he felt that he could not stand the strain much longer. He was flying on his nerves, and he knew it. His flying was getting wild and erratic.

Turning, he swerved into the side of the cloud, temporarily blinding himself, and then burst out again, fighting frantically to keep the machine under control. Bullets were crashing into his engine, and he wondered why it did not burst into flames.

157

Where were the bullets coming from? He leaned over the side of the cockpit and looked behind. A yellow Hun was on his tail. He turned with a speed that amazed himself. Unprepared for the move, the Hun overshot him. Next instant the tables were turned, Biggles roaring down after the Triplane in hot pursuit.

Rat-tat-tat-tat! stuttered his guns. At such short range it was impossible to miss. The yellow top wing swung back and floated away into space; the fuselage plunged out of sight, a streamer of flame creeping along its side. For a moment Biggles watched it, fascinated, then he looked up with a start. Where were the others? Where were the Camels? He was just in time to see one of them disappear into the side of the cloud, then he was alone.

At first he could not believe it. Where were the Huns? Not one was in sight. Where, a moment or two before, there had been twenty or more machines, not one remained except himself—yes, one; a Camel was just disappearing through the floor of the basin.

A feeling of horrible loneliness came over him and a doubt crept into his mind as to his ability to find his way home. He had not the remotest idea of his position. He looked upwards, but from his own level to the distant circle of blue at the top of the crater there was not a single machine to be seen. He had hoped to see the F.E. that had had disappeared into the mist come out again, but it did not.

I'll bet that Camel pilot knows where he is; I'll go after him, he thought desperately, and tore down in the wake of the single-seater that had disappeared below. He looked at his altimeter, which had somehow escaped the general ruin caused by the bullets. One thousand feet, it read. He sank into the mist and came out under it almost at once. Below lay open country—fields, hedges, and a long, deserted road. Not a soul was in sight as far as he could see, and there was no landmark that he could recognize.

He saw the Camel. It was still going down, and he raced after it, intending to get alongside in the hope of making his predicament known to the pilot. Then, with a shock of understanding, he saw that the Camel's propeller was not turning. Its engine must have been put out of action in the combat and the pilot had no alternative to landing.

As he watched the machine he saw the leather-helmeted head turn in the cockpit as the pilot looked back over his shoulder. Then the head turned again and the machine made a neat landing in a field.

Biggles did not hesitate. He knew they were far over hostile country—how far he did not like to think—and the Camel pilot must be rescued. The wrecked 'plane was blazing when he landed beside it, and its pilot ran towards him, carrying a still smoking Very pistol in his hand. Biggles recognized him. 'Mahoney!' he yelled.

The Camel pilot pulled up dead and stared. 'Great Scott!' he cried. 'If it isn't Biggles!'

'Get aboard, and buck up about it!' shouted Biggles.

Mahoney clambered aboard, and perched himself close behind Biggles, hanging on for dear life. 'Look out!' he yelled. 'Huns!'

Biggles did not look. He saw little tufts of grass flying up just in front of the machine, and he heard the rattle of a gun. It told him all he needed to know, and he knew he had no time to lose.

The machine took a long run to get off with its unusual burden, but it managed it. Fortunately, its nose was pointing towards the Lines, and there was no need to turn. The machine zoomed upwards and the mist enfolded them like a blanket.

For a few minutes Biggles fought his way through the gloom; then he put the nose of the machine down again, for he knew he could not hope to keep it on even keel for very long in such conditions. The ground loomed darkly below; he corrected the machine, and then climbed up again. 'Do you know where we are?' he yelled.

Mahoney nodded, and made a sign that he was to keep straight on.

Biggles breathed more comfortably, and flew along just at the base of the clouds.

Mahoney guided him to the aerodrome, and after a bumpy landing, the aircraft ran to a standstill in front of

No. 266 Squadron sheds, where a number of officers and mechanics were watching.

There was a general babble of excitement in which everybody talked at once. Biggles was warmly congratulated on his rescue work, which everyone present regarded as an exceptionally good show.

'Does anyone know what happened to the two F.E.s?' he asked.

'Yes, they've gone home,' said several voices at once. 'They broke off the fight when we did, and we all came home together.'

'Thank goodness!' muttered Biggles. 'I thought they'd all gone west.'

'Well, it was a bonny dog-fight!' sighed Mahoney. 'The sort of scrap one remembers. Hallo, here's the C.O. Hi, sir,' he called, 'Bigglesworth picked me up this morning in Hunland after a Boche had shot my engine to scrap iron.'

Major Mullen shot a glance at Biggles, noting his white face and trembling hands. He knew the signs. He had seen them too often not to recognize them. The pitcher can go too often to the well, and, as he knew from grim experience, the best of nerves cannot indefinitely stand the strain of air combat.

'Good show, Bigglesworth!' he said calmly. 'Go and have a rest, then report to me later.'

Mahoney glanced quickly at Biggles, seemed about to say something, then thought better of it and passed on his way.

Several hours later Biggles stood before Major Mullen, who regarded him sympathetically.

'Feeling the strain a bit, aren't you?' queried the C.O.

'No, sir,' said Biggles desperately.

But the major shook his head. 'Yes, you are. You can't fool me, my lad. We've all got our limits. You've done better than most of us, but you've got to have a real rest. I promised you a week's leave to go and see Mark Way. Well, take it, and forget flying for a bit. You'll come back all the better for it. Cheerio, and the best of luck!'

Biggles gripped his commander's hand, saluted, and went off to pack his things.